If I Knew Then
What I Know Now

Our Quest for Quality of Life

Doreen L. Guma, MA, FACHE, CPC, CLC

Introduction

❧

Hard Life?

*W*ho makes it hard? Let me save you all the finger pointing and get right to the answer. YOU DO. That's pretty much it in a nutshell.

I absolutely know that I have made my life harder than it has had to be. I know we were put on this earth to learn and to have experiences, good and bad. That is how we grow.

In this book, my colleagues and I are privileged to tell our stories. Through these chapters you will hear what we have learned in our lives and some observations that we have identified along the way.

Hopefully, something we have learned pertains to something that you are going through. It is my hope that one of the things we have learned will be pertinent in your life and can save you some time. Maybe it can help you make a small change so you will not be forty-five or fifty-five or sixty-five and think, "I should have . . . ." After all, a different way of thinking or one small change has the potential to make your life better.

It is my prayer that this book will bring you hope and resources. It's time to Enjoy YOUR Life.

Author's Note:

❧

This book, while there are references to God, is meant to be non-denominational and to speak to anyone who values the powerful message in the statement of "If I knew then what I know now".

In this book we speak of our journeys in life and tell our stories of what we have learned. These stories may include a writer's personal beliefs and thoughts and are not intended to impose personal viewpoints on others. It is up to each individual to form their own beliefs and their own opinions.

Our stories are from our heart, and are our gift to you, with the hope to help you enjoy your life.

Dedication

༺❀༻

I dedicate this book to my husband, James, a retired New York City Police Sergeant who has seen people in the best and worst times of life. He always maintains a positive outlook towards life and finding the best in people and every situation. He enjoys life and always makes "Time to Play". I thank him for always being there and supporting me in all of my endeavors, even though he cringes every time I say, "I've been thinking." I thank him for being my best friend and teaching me to see beauty in the world.

I truly, from the bottom of my heart, thank all of my contributors for their belief in this project. I thank Morgan for all her hard work in editing to make our stories shine.

I thank my children, Gregory, Nicholas and Jacquelyn for forgiving me if I was distant while fighting my internal battles. I will always love and be proud of each of you, forever.

I thank my whole family, especially my mother for not giving up and trying her best, my mother and father-in-law for "adopting me", and my sisters Gayle and Stacy and my brother Jonathan who I know are always there if I need them.

Finally, and most importantly, I thank God for providing me with His guidance. For without Him planting the seed for this book in my mind those nine years ago, it would never have gotten started. I give Him all the credit for guiding it to completion in what I now realize was His perfect timing.

Contents

꧁

N *ote: The chapters in this book follow the Time to Play Philosophy with sections on Happiness, Health, Money and Work Life Balance. Each chapter's contributor has been listed following the chapter's title.*

Happy Reading!

Contents

Section 1

Happiness

ᢋᢤᢇ

"Smile. You have the ability to make your life AMAZING." ~ Doreen Guma

Chapter 1

No Simple Solution

༄

I am a believer that anything and everything has an opportunity for improvement. I also believe that people have the ability to be happy, healthy, have money and a work life balance. That is why I founded TimetoPlay.com, a place to find resources for a better life, so we can all enjoy life.

My vision is to create some positive in our world. Sure, there is good news out there when I look around, and *sometimes* there is a feel-good story when I watch the news. However, I find the majority of the news negative, high-lighting inconceivable atrocities against others. It almost seems that some media scour to find the most horrific events possible to report on. The daily dose of the many negative and dishonest events we hear about truly hurts my soul. When it came time for Jim and I to discuss having children, we reflected on this daily barrage of how bad things seemed to be, how hard it may be for our children growing up, and what they may face. I asked him if he was sure he wanted to bring someone in to this world and he replied that yes, he did, as maybe one of them would be able to fix it.

While all three of my children have amazing qualities, and I cannot be prouder of them, I acknowledge that not one person can possibly "fix" what ails our society. Some time ago I was speaking with an administrator in our school district and this topic came up. During our discussion, she voiced that she did not believe there was one simple solution to what ails our society. I have been pondering this issue for quite some time, and frequently think about her statement. No, I do not believe there is one simple solution. There are many different issues, life concerns, and situations that individually affect our people. While I acknowledge that our earthly experience is truly individual to that person, their mindset, their physical condition, their drive, and their passion, one common phrase has to remain true.

"Where there's a will, there's a way"

When put into perspective, perhaps, there **is** one simple solution and the potential for a "meeting of the minds". I believe it is possible to find a common will to actually bring about changes for the betterment of all. I believe it is possible for things to change for the better, for people to not complain, to not point fingers, and to not perceive obstacles as impossible to conquer.

In my past experience as chair of many different committees, one of the most perplexing things to me has been how people sometimes just make up their minds without, perhaps, seeing the bigger picture. It is important to consider how <u>anything</u> that happens will somehow impact others – like dominoes. In relation to my dream to help people and for Time to Play in general, people have critiqued that it is not possible to change everything. First, I no longer believe there is *anything* in this world that is completely impossible. Second, it is not my intention to "fix" everything. However, I do believe it is possible to motivate others to see the brighter side in life. I have noticed that many people have adopted a negative or hopeless outlook, but I believe **<u>every</u>** individual has the power within to find happiness and make their life amazing. The key is that, **individually**, each person has to know in their heart that they possess the unique potential to be anything. They need to believe they can achieve and do anything they set their mind to. I find this statement by Eleanor Roosevelt to be very true, "Life is what you make it. Always has been, always will be."

I recently had the privilege to speak in my daughter's class. I told the high school students why I care. I told the students the story of my concern about my own three children growing up in what we hear as being a "hard society". Is there less opportunity today? Less jobs? Less people in the middle class? The negative news or negative projections might make people feel there is no opportunity, or "why bother". I truly still believe America remains the land of opportunity and that you have to believe in yourself to make things happen. We have to recapture our power and never give up. It is written in Mark 9:23, **"As far as possibilities go, everything is possible for the person who believes"**. Not growing up in faith, it has taken me too long to believe in this philosophy. It has also taken a long time for me to believe in myself.

I also discussed with the students my belief of how it is important for people to work together to make things better for everyone, that we must unite to make things change. I emphasized that I believe this is important, not just for my own children, but for all children. When you think about it, every child out there is like our own child. Every child that hurts does affect us in some way. Furthermore, you can apply this concept to every person on this planet. For every person that suffers it somehow affects our lives. We are all connected, and I believe it is our duty and responsibility to make improvements so we can all have a better life.

As you read this book you will find that I am very opinionated. You might agree with me, or you might not. Hopefully you can see a little piece of truth or identify with stories written in this book. My goal for *If I Knew Then What I Know Now* is to help me, you, and others – people helping people – make our lives better.

One of the most important things I want to communicate, something I became aware of through my own life experience, is how difficult it may be for someone to identify that they are in situation they can change to lead a more fulfilled life. We may "think" we are happy, or we may realize we are not happy but cannot put our finger on why. Sometimes we know why but are not ready to change things. Sometimes we do not realize our lives can be better, or that we may be living in an experience where we are just going through the motions of our day. This is where I found myself. On the proverbial hamster wheel, losing track of the days. Did you ever realize how fast the days, weeks, months, and years, just fly by?

And then I was forty-five years old, looking around and wondering how I became so serious. How did I forget how to have fun? How did I not know how to "let go"? How did I forget to notice the little things? In those days I described myself as boring and very "corporate". Always business, always doing stuff, always on a schedule, always thinking about the next thing I needed to do, and the years flew by. I realized this was no longer the way I wanted to live, and embarked on my "quest for quality of life" with my primary goal to relearn how to enjoy life. Since starting on my journey I realized there are others out there like me. I invite you to embark on your own personal journey to learn what you need to achieve quality of life.

Again, while I realize it is not my, or anyone else's, responsibility to "fix" others or to fix our society, it is my intention to plant a seed in the reader's mind here or on the Time to Play website to, perhaps, initiate a change in their lives. Maybe just a small change, one that might even feel insignificant, but just might be all that is needed to turn things around for the better. Since I believe we are all somehow connected, when one person changes for the better, their change may affect others or their surroundings, as well. Ever hear the analogy of the "pebble in the pond"? You never know how big the ripples can become that can touch many other people.

In writing this book I have asked for contributions from relatives, friends and others I have met along the way. It is a sharing of our experiences and a reflection on what we have learned.

While I know that making mistakes are a part of life, it is my hope that through our stories we might save you some time so you are not forty-five or fifty-five or seventy-five and realize that you could have done something earlier. It is my hope our words may spark a change, a new awareness, or a different path for you. I personally do not plan to get to the end of my life with regrets, and I cannot imagine there are any people out there who want that for themselves, either.

There is no better day to start living and making your life better as this very one.

It is time to **Enjoy YOUR Life!**

Chapter 2

We Are All Tortured Souls

❧

"Who am I to write this book"? That is the statement I woke up with running through my mind this morning. It did not end there. The little voice kept at me. Who am I to think I can write a book? I am not a psychologist or a psychiatrist. I am just a little 5 foot 2 inch woman from Long Island with a vision of hope. Hope that, perhaps, someone reading this book will identify with something we have written. Hope that they realize they are in an undesirable situation where they feel unhappy, displeased, hopeless, or helpless. Hope that what we have written might spark a change so they can live a better life.

But, still, I ask. . . what do I know of the plight of others? What makes me special? What makes me able to do this? Is there real validity in what I want to achieve? Are my opinions and observations justified?

<u>Why do we do this to ourselves?</u>

I have come to the conclusion that we are all tortured souls. But, it is my opinion that we do it to ourselves. How many of us have woken up exhausted because we have tossed and turned at night. It is the things we cannot let go in our minds that keep us up. It is the things we allow to take our precious moments away and that do not allow us to rest.

"No rest for the weary" ~ Unknown

No rest for our thoughts that poison our happiness. Not while we are awake, not while we are asleep. I have found myself awake many a night at three o'clock a.m. with my heart pounding out of my chest. Why? I was worried <u>ABOUT EVERYTHING</u>. I let things that happened during my day take away my power. Does this happen to you?

Over these past few years I have been reading a lot. In the book *The Power of Positive Thinking* by Dr. Norman Vincent Peale, first published in 1952, he wrote that 50 – 75% of people were ill because they were filled with fear, anxiety, tension, resentment, guilt, or a combination of all of these. He also noted that people may be suffering with pains and aches because of what is bothering them emotionally.[1] My simplification? People allow what is in their minds to torture them. To emphasize my point, Dr. Peale's book was written over **sixty** years ago. When I read Dr. Peale's book I was **amazed** by his statistics on the number of people <u>at</u>

<u>that time</u> on antidepressants and sleep aids. I bet he would not believe today's statistics regarding the number of people suffering from depression or on antidepressant medications. When you look at today's statistics on depression, divorce or suicide, one cannot help but think that we are somehow doing something wrong in our society. Since reading Dr. Peale's book, I have wondered how we could have ignored such findings and allowed things to progress to what is happening today. Based on the many published articles and statistics available on this topic, it is evident that many people must feel stressed, frustrated or otherwise victimized.

I find what is worse is that very few people discuss these things. It may be embarrassing to say that you are having problems sleeping because of stress, and, if you do, the first thing your physician may want to do is to put you on medication. Or, perhaps we believe that if we tell someone we are troubled we might show a sign of weakness, and our pride will just not allow that, right? Without generalizing, I have simplified my concept by labeling us as a band aid society. Instead of fixing our situations, we just look for the easy way out. Sometimes the easy way is not only <u>not</u> the best way, but a bad way. This does not just apply to negative thoughts that may haunt us, but is meant to describe the way we address issues that affect us across the board.

Perhaps we should talk about our problems or learn from those who have "been down the same road". I am sure many things we face today are things people have experienced in the past. That is the point of this book, "if I knew then what

I know now". Unfortunately, we sometimes do know but we may choose to ignore a situation. As it relates to negative feelings or thoughts, I now realize the first step is to recognize you have negative feelings or thoughts in the first place. Then, and only then, can you begin to search for the root cause.

I have spent many years working in the field of quality improvement. It is my belief that, no matter what the situation is, things can always be better. Even if you are the CEO of a multi-million dollar business, or you have the perfect family, or job, etc., you can always improve on something. Again, the first step is to identify something that can be improved. In this case it may be that little voice or the negativity we allow in our lives. Then we can begin to look for the root cause and what is causing the "voices" in the first place. I want to emphasize that I believe we **enable** ourselves to be "tortured souls". I believe we allow ourselves to be disempowered or have negative thoughts – but, there is a bright side. **<u>WE</u>** have the power to stop them and to change our situation.

"Next time you are stressed, take a step back, inhale and laugh. Remember who you are and why you are here. You are never given anything in this world that you cannot handle. Be strong, be flexible, love yourself, and love others. Always remember, just keep moving forward" ~ Unknown

This is a great quote to really start us on our journey. In my quest for quality of life, I have read and searched and researched. I have talked to people and heard their stories of how they changed their lives.

We may be tortured souls, but it is up to us to take the torture and use it as positive motivation to change things to make our lives better. It is also our choice to allow negative beliefs or feelings to overtake us and create negative, self-destructive behaviors. When faced with a negative situation, some of us become responsible, strong and motivated, while others become victims. Some of us rise to victory while some allow others to intimidate and manipulate us, further creating our downward spiral in life.

How many among us fall into the trap of letting someone take our power, even briefly. Over the years, working on my "quest for quality of life", I now realize the affect people and what their opinions have had on me. I am thankful that I now realize it when someone makes me feel bad or steals my power. It might take a few hours or a day to snap out of it, whereas, in the past, it would take much longer and affect me much more deeply.

Words Cut Like a Knife

What do you say to people? Do you encourage them? Discourage them? Tell them that they are stupid? That their dreams are stupid? That they will not amount to anything? That they are never going to make it?

Are you a parent, coworker, boss, teacher, sister, brother, or student? Did you ever do this? Did you see the hurt you instilled in the other person when you looked into their eyes? Do you know what your words might have done to them?

Words are power. What we choose to say can make the biggest difference in another person's life - for the better or for the worse. I happened upon Joel Osteen recently. I watch him, no pun intended, quite religiously every week, and wait anxiously for the messages and words of wisdom he sends to my email or posts on the internet. He has great insight into the negative, disempowering thinking that many people partake in, and I believe that he is very empowering. Recently he said something that jarred my memory about a common phrase I grew up with,

**"If you do not have anything nice to say,
do not say it at all"** ~ Unknown

Remember that one? What happened to that principal? I believe we would be better off if we adopted this awareness in today's society. Think of the news, the bullying, the political races, or even what we say or think about ourselves. Instead, what if we started to say nice, positive things about ourselves and each other?

Be a cheerleader

Growing up, during high school, I was a cheerleader. As part of the cheerleading squad it was our job to keep the people watching the game and the players hopeful. It was our job to promote the games, to create "a hoopla", to bring excitement to the other students. No matter what our team's season looked like, we wore our uniforms the day of the game around the school. We made signs with the player's names on them. We decorated lockers for both the players and the other cheerleaders. We brought hope to our schoolmates. Look back at your life experience. Were you a cheerleader or did you hate the cheerleaders? Were you supportive of the players? Maybe we do our best, and maybe we have "demons" within that we have to fight. Maybe we do not feel we are "good enough", a topic we will get to later. Think of the possibilities if we all became part of the same team.

I have lived my life as a cheerleader. I have always encouraged others in every job I have ever had. A job is different when you believe in an organization's mission and what their goals are, not just go to a job, perform the required motions and complain you hate the job and hate going to work. This concept can be applied to every area of our lives. We can enjoy our day or we can complain.

When I meet people, I listen to their passion, what they are working on, and what they believe in. When I can, I will support their goals and what is in their heart. If they are "down in the dumps", I try to help then, too. I know we are all born with a gift, and that we all have something to offer that can help someone else. Maybe it is as simple as giving advice, telling about an experience we have had or something we have learned. It is up to us if we choose to use our gifts and knowledge to help others, or if we choose to stay quiet and in the background. Through Time To Play, I have been blessed with opportunities to meet professionals and others who have experience that can benefit others. I love to hear their stories and have been in awe of them and their undying motivation to make a difference. However, not all of whom I have met while working on this project have had the same motivation. There are the "what is in it for me" people, who will be discussed, too.

I cannot say the way I choose to live is not exhausting. I know that, many times, I have not reciprocally gotten back support from others after I have supported them. When you look back at your motivation for participating in something, I have learned that it should not solely be based on what you will get back in return. It might be more of what the outcome of your contribution could be or what your participation can help improve, even if it is just making another person feel good for that moment. I have learned that participating in something when you expect something in return will, many times, leave you frustrated, disappointed, and unfulfilled.

"Give. Keep giving. And expect nothing in return"
~ Unknown

Did I always believe this? Nope. Of course I have what I call the "helping sickness". I always want to help. Everybody. I truly find pleasure in helping make someone else's life better. But, now I help and then move on to the next thing I can do to help somewhere else. I do not help and wait to get something back, because "something" might never happen. It takes time to realize this, but it frees you up to go on, move to the next project, event or person, and to help some more.

As a cheerleader, it is up to me to see the good in what another person has to offer, to make them feel good about themselves, and to offer them encouragement that may build their confidence and self-esteem. Take a moment to look inside yourself and what you do in your life today. Do you see the beauty in others, their talents, or their value? Are you a cheerleader?

If I knew then what I know now, I would not change being a cheerleader throughout my life. You do not have the time, you say? None of us have time, but people can always find time to do something if they really want to. Sometimes you will hear people say they are tired of helping, that when they help they always get a "slap in the face". For those people, I think it is time to review their initial motivation in the first place.

Something to consider is the potential to spread ourselves too thin. I know I have done this to a point of where I have sacrificed quality of life for myself and my family. I now realize we do need to make priorities and to pick and choose to participate in what is most important to us. We cannot do everything. But, I believe we are all put on this Earth to help each other. Deeply rooted in what I believe is the founding principle behind Time to Play: *People Helping People*. I believe in the need to support each other. We have all heard the ideal that we are all connected. Without generalizing too much, I would go so far as to say that a valid cause supported by one person somehow affects all of us in some way.

My next discussion can potentially insult someone. However, remember I am here pouring out my soul, what I have observed and what I believe. I am not intending to insult anyone, and am taking a chance by generalizing to note another expression that someone, somewhere, stated. We have heard it and we have said it, or at least I know I have.

Do you share a big vision? Do you look at a bigger picture, or are you stuck in your own bubble, with your own problems, in your own world. In my experience, I know that is where I had been for a long time. Stuck in my own bubble making . . . **mountains out of molehills** (this will be further discussed in my chapter, *Always Striving for the Brass Ring*). Ever hear this phrase:

"Cannot see beyond/past the end of your nose"

Let me digress a moment. It amazes me that someone, somewhere, said these "words of wisdom" that caught on and have been passed down generation to generation. We say them, we tell them to others, we continue to pass them on; but what do we do to change our reoccurring actions reflected in these sayings? I am guilty of this as much as anyone else, but am always excited when I come up with one of these expressions. In writing this chapter I realize I would say the chosen "words of wisdom" and then move on. My intention for the future is to now recognize them as a trigger, a lesson in what is being said, where there is an opportunity to learn something. Stopping a moment to evaluate what prompted the expression may prove helpful to move forward or make things better for ourselves and others.

On with that story I was going to tell. I was the president of our Civic Association for many years. The goal of the Civic Association was to make the lives better for the members of our community, as a whole. The Civic came up with a slogan, "neighbor helping neighbor". Like those before me, there was frustration by the officers who would get 25 to 40 people to come to our monthly meetings out of the over 8,000 families in our community. We did the best we could to educate and inform others about the happenings in our community and issues that affected us. Unfortunately, unless something <u>DIRECTLY</u> affected a person who lived in our community, or their home, or their block, they would not come out to support the Civic Association to improve quality of life for all of us. Most of the time people came, we fought for what they needed help with, and after, they were gone.

I remained an officer of the Civic for years and finally stopped actively participating after what I experienced at a town board meeting. We had been trying to get people to look at zoning in our community so that what would be built in the future would compliment, not negatively impact, the quality of life for us all. At that meeting, people who never attended our meetings but lived in our community were fighting against a proposed six month building moratorium. The reason the moratorium was being requested by the Civic Association and the person who was hired to complete the study was so that the community would remain as it was until the unused areas were reviewed for potential zoning changes or recommendations. The person who was most memorable was a woman who lived in our community and was fighting against the moratorium. She was upset that, with the moratorium, her then one year old child would not be able to build a house on the property they bought on an adjoining lot to her home, which was the reason they purchased the property. Let me remind you, it was a six month moratorium, not a moratorium on building forever. That is when I realized people in my community were not looking out for each other. We were striving independently, without seeing past the end of our noses. I began to apply this realization to other situations where it was evident people went with the flow instead of truly understanding the situation at hand.

That brings me to an observation I read in the book, *I Dare You*, by William H. Danforth. He originally published this book in 1953. Like Dr. Peale's book, I think it is very interesting to again emphasize that observations made years ago could help us today. In his chapter, *Launch Out Into the Deep*, Mr. Danforth noted that 95% of the people are content to go along their own way, that 4% are leaders, and that only 1% reach the top. He noted how the 95% have unused capacities that can be tapped. Are you part of the 95% just following along not reaching your potential? Do you listen to others without looking at the big picture? Are you a voice of reason or change making things better for everyone, or just trapped inside your own bubble?

Again, this observation was not meant to insult anyone, but an observation I realized after many years of personal sacrifice. I never asked for anything in return, and was proud to help and to serve. I do look back now, knowing I did my best, but will always remain perplexed. I know people are so busy in their lives, but when did we stop watching out for each other? This is not intended to be a full generalization of our whole society. Perhaps this is indicative of an isolated incident that is not the norm. I recognize that there are an insurmountable number of issues out there. I realize that people are sometimes overwhelmed just getting through their day and taking care of their immediate needs. However, this was my experience over a ten year period. Again, over these ten years people came with their own agendas, we fought, then they disappeared. I always have said that, if a road had to go through the middle of my house, but that it was the best option for the majority, I would support the project. Maybe my broad way of thinking is against the general norm, but I hate to think so. I always will continue to strive forward with the vision of neighbor helping neighbor and people helping people with the hope that, in the future, we can work together more cohesively and not just worry what is happening in our immediate lives.

With that, another expression comes to mind:

"All for One, One for All"

I remember this from the Three Musketeers, but if you research it there are other origins. For the purpose of this discussion, I wonder if the philosophy behind the expression is possible to achieve. It is sad for me to say, but since starting the Time to Play project I have met many people with a "what is in it for me" attitude. If you look around, in our society, it seems that this is really a big motivating factor. "If I will look good, then I will do it". In the past I had advised my kids to participate in something because it would look good on their resume. I now realize that the most important part of participating is because it feels like the right thing to do.

Working in healthcare, one of my biggest pet peeves is how people care about a particular disease process only after it affects them directly, if they or their loved one gets cancer, Alzheimer's, multiple sclerosis, etc. You get the idea. What about the people that are affected by these situations every day? What about those who need blood, food, and more? Collaboratively, I believe we can shift anything. I know there is a solution to every problem, but solutions are dependent on our motivation to work together to make things happen; to care enough about others and their plight.

With that, I leave you to ponder the concept of people helping people and "all for one, one for all". After all, it has to be our responsibility to make the world a better place for everyone.

Chapter 3

Quality of Life

ᦉᦉ

Contributor: Rebecca L. Norrington

*T*he chances that Rebecca and I would have ever met in this lifetime were more than one in a billion. Rebecca is on the West Coast, and I am on the East Coast. I was a guest on an Internet radio show that she had never listened to before which she had just happened upon. On the radio show I was discussing Time to Play's philosophy and explaining how it provides resources so people can learn what they need in order to enjoy life. Rebecca shares many of my beliefs and philosophies and contacted me that same day. We have spoken for hours on end and have visited together when we are in the same state. We became fast friends, and she has become part of my core team. Rebecca is an amazing resource on how to achieve happiness in our lives. She encourages all in her path. Her words of wisdom pick you up and strengthen you to believe in yourself. With strength, belief and faith, we know that anything we desire to achieve is possible.

I am very grateful that Rebecca came into my life. I have learned so much from her, and her chapter is a gift to us. She and I share the philosophy that WE create the circumstances of our daily life, that we are responsible for our behavior, and that our negative or positive reactions to a situation tremendously affect us. I truly appreciate the heart-felt information she shares on how to forgive, and she, herself, is first hand proof that forgiveness can free one's soul.

I thank Rebecca for sharing what she has learned and what she now knows. I hope you enjoy reading her chapter and that you will choose to apply some of her simple steps to attain quality in YOUR life.

— *Dawn*

What does "Quality of Life" mean to you? It is an important question that can only be answered by someone special. . . **and that someone special is YOU!**

You, and you alone, have the ability to create a barometer for living a quality life. I would like to share with you what I consider to be a few principal components in maintaining my own "quality of life" status. It is difficult to list everything

I consider imperative to living a life of quality; however I have chosen a few of my favorite topics including: What is Important, Defining Energy, The Power of Forgiveness, The Truth Between Inside and Outside Priorities, Your Perspective (an important factor), and the Gift of Life. I believe all of these are fundamental components to achieving a Life of Quality, and I hope you enjoy reading what I have learned.

What does the statement "Quality of Life" mean to you? I believe that what determines "quality of life" is different to every single person reading this. What defines **your** "quality of life" depends solely on your personal perspective. Since your experiences are unique to you, it is impossible for you to perceive things exactly the way I would, or vice-versa, and that is okay. In fact, that is more than okay, because now we can exchange ideas with less conflict and struggle.

Think about our differences like this: We all have a set of fingerprints, and with that said, we are all as *different* as our fingerprints. When you begin to *accept* the differences of others, the quality of your life will change. When I began to practice accepting the differences between my fellow "cohabitants," the quality of my life dramatically improved. I began to listen with different *ears*. Instead of spending valuable time arguing my point and trying to convince others that my opinion is the only one that matters, I spent my time accepting other people's opinions. This does not mean I changed my opinion. It just means that I do not spend MY TIME trying to convince others that my opinion is right. Think about it. How many times have you been in an argument with someone and mid-way through they stopped and said, "Oh, my God, you are right! I did not know what I was thinking. Thank GOD you shared YOUR opinion with me because I have been wrong all this time!" Has that ever happened to you? I used to spend time trying to convince somebody else of what I think, and then had to listen to what they think, and then I would present my side again. . . and they would offer a rebuttal. . . ARGH! I realize that I have literally spent years campaigning for my opinion to be accepted as the world's opinion. Our differences are what make our glorious world go around. Practice accepting differences without disagreeing with them and your quality of life will improve.

Through my own personal growth, I have learned that what I used to think would add to the quality of my life significantly changed. I have also learned that what we view as important to our "quality of life" automatically changes over time. Despite how you choose to define "quality of life" for yourself today, know that it may eventually change tomorrow.

What Is So Important? Years ago I volunteered as an activity director in an assisted-living home. I was given an opportunity to spend two hours each week planning activities like chair aerobics, sing-a-longs, simple games, etc. As you can imagine, the age of the majority of residents were in their seventies, eighties, and nineties.

I remember thinking all of these people have been fortunate enough to make it to this stage in their lives, and I became curious to find out more about each person. Specifically, what did a seventy, eighty, or ninety-year-old think was important? I was in my thirties at the time, and I was sure that what I thought was important was not important to them. So, I did what I always do when I want information: I asked. The following week I decided to schedule an hour to listen to what my new friends wanted in their lives. I wanted to learn what really was important to them. I arranged some chairs in a circle so that everyone was able to have eye contact with one another. I asked them, one by one, "If you could have anything in the world, what would it be?" I walked around the circle repeating this question to each of the twenty-five seated people.

The majority of the people wanted better health. A few people wanted a companion. Some expressed a desire to travel. One woman's response was unforgettable. She said, "I want my own car. I want to be able to drive again." Of course, I needed to ask her the million-dollar follow-up question, "Why?" She replied, "I don't see my daughter anymore because she moved to another city forty-five minutes away. She doesn't visit me as often as she used to, and if I had my own car, I would be able to drive to see her." Her answer made a profound impact on my life; from that day forward, I consciously made changes as to what I thought was really important in my life. Her answer changed the frequency of my interactions with my parents. In fact, when my parents retired and moved 275 miles away, I visited them more than when they lived in town.

"Quality of Life changes with time and experience."
~ Rebecca L. Norrington

The Quality of Your Life Depends on Your Energy: Everything is made up of energy. Let me re-emphasize that. . . **everything**. Energy can be transformed into other forms of energy, but energy alone cannot be created AND it cannot be destroyed. Energy will always exist in one form or another. Everything we do, think, and say involves some type of energy. Our personal spirit, our thoughts, our bodies, and our emotions are all energy. In fact, everything that happens in the Universe, from a volcano erupting to a seed sprouting, to people walking and talking, takes energy.

In recent years, science has discovered that every person on the planet possesses what is known as a personal energy frequency, or *vibration*. This *personal vibration* dictates what kind of circumstances and events we attract into our lives. How? Because **like** energy attracts **like** energy. It is really quite simple. Whatever frequency we are vibrating at attracts **like** vibrations. Our personal vibration is an invisible but powerful force that determines our life experiences. Whether we know it or not, the truth is, we all have the power to *choose* our vibration. Some people choose by default, some people choose by habit, and some choose consciously.

I love to explain this concept with an analogy of listening to the radio. When you listen to the radio, you choose a channel. Your choice depends on what you want to hear. Whatever station you choose has a distinct frequency or vibration. What is your favorite station? Which station do you tune into during the day? ANGER 97.3? Moodiness 101.3? Blaming 87.5? Complaining 105.7? Judging All 640? Worry, Worry, Worry in a Hurry 790?

There is an easy way to discover your favorite stations. Keep a pen and paper with you during the day and jot down how you are feeling every half hour. Do this throughout the day for twenty-four hours. This fun, easy exercise will assist you in determining how, what, when and why you are feeling a certain way. This exercise serves as practice to begin living consciously—as opposed to living habitually. And, the good news is, there are no penalties for getting angry or blaming or even being judgmental. This exercise is merely a beginner's guide to living consciously, because when you begin to live consciously, your life changes. Living consciously means you have more choices of behavior to choose from. Living consciously means you choose how you want to feel. Living consciously means you choose your vibration! *Your personal vibration is extremely important in determining your quality of life.*

The fact that energy or vibrations can influence a person's reality is nothing new. Throughout history, different cultures have recognized and developed ways to work with self-energy. The Chinese practice Tai Chi; in India, people practice Kundalini; and in Japan, Reiki. All three practices focus on personal energy.

If your personal vibration is "low", then you are more likely to exhibit anger, become moody, worry, stress, or be anxious while feeling sad, depressed, neglected, discouraged, fearful, alone, etc. While emitting a lower vibration or frequency you will never really experience a peaceful and happy life. . . it is impossible. Like developing any skill, it is not easy to raise your vibration over night. Raising your vibration requires a daily unwavering commitment from you, but trust me, it is worth it.

When your personal vibration is "high", you are more likely to feel optimistic, grateful, competent, confidant, purposeful, valued, appreciated, LOVED, and connected. When you are able to maintain a high personal vibration, you develop the ability to be happy regardless of external circumstances. In addition, your thoughts and behaviors have more **effectiveness** when you act from a positive state as opposed to a negative one. An added bonus is that your positive energy, along with your higher vibration, acts as a ripple effect throughout the world. Because you have raised your vibration, you have actually made the world a better place without even leaving home.

FORGIVENESS: The subject of forgiveness is one of my favorite topics. Who has not been in a situation that requires forgiving someone? In my opinion, when you choose not to forgive and, more importantly, choose not to forgive *quickly*, you might as well drink a cup of poison every day of your life until you make the selfish choice to forgive. Yes, true forgiveness is selfish. It seems odd to say, but when you choose to forgive, you are acting in your best interest. Of course the other person benefits from your actions; however, you are the person receiving the most benefit. When I finally realized that forgiveness has nothing to do with another person—that forgiveness is a gift that keeps on giving to **Self,** I was sold.

Let me share a few personal stories. While growing up I witnessed a lot of behaviors that taught me how I was *supposed* to act if I felt slighted or wronged. None of the behaviors I observed were an immediate act of forgiveness. When my mother and father argued, their behavior was always followed by what I called "punishment". My father would give my mother the "cold shoulder" and not speak to her for days. Honestly, looking back, I did not know there were other choices I could have made. It was not until I met my now ex-husband that I learned that a couple was supposed to "talk out" their problems and "never go to bed angry". My husband might as well have been speaking a foreign language when he explained this to me. Not only did I find the concept of working problems out a problem in itself, but believed that any type of compromise was a sign of weakness!

During my most impressionable years I witnessed my father and his *only* brother ostracize each other for over more than a decade. They had a falling out over how to manage an apartment building they both owned. Over the years I have since realized the real problem was not how they needed to manage the apartment building, but how they managed their relationship. I believe, in most families, the real problems are unresolved issues that may have arisen during childhood.

I recall a grandmother who banished her son because of the woman he chose to marry. All of my life I have watched mothers, fathers, siblings, aunts, uncles, and cousins, engage in "you're dead to me" behavior. So, it is understandable I adopted the same type of social skills.

Yes, I have indulged in off-and-on relationships with people for years. Childhood friends, relatives, in-laws, co-workers, boyfriends, students, the list is quite extensive. I honestly did not know that: (1) I could choose a different type of behavior than the one I learned early in my life, and (2) I was harming myself both physically and emotionally with my behaviors. Just like Dorothy from the *Wizard of Oz*, I had the power to create whatever type of relationship I wanted, but I did not know that. . . until now.

A year before my father died, my mother disinherited me for reasons she believed are just, and chose not to speak to or see me for years. At this point, I have not seen my mother in over five years, which I hope to change in the near future. Interestingly enough, even though I remain disinherited, we speak to each other nearly every day. I make it a point to end every conversation with a heartfelt, "I love you, Mommy!" Have you ever heard of a child who was disinherited and kept the lines of communication open with the parent who disinherited them? I have not. It is really simple: If I choose to harbor bad feelings, I am choosing toxic behavior. I have never known toxic behavior to result in anything good. Have you?

Forgive As Fast As You Can: For most people a decision to forgive comes, if ever, at the end of a long emotional journey that may stretch over months, if not years. I will admit, for the majority of my life, forgiving was not on my "things to do" list. However, when I found out the truth about the benefits of forgiveness, I began practicing the skill immediately. I was able to forgive my mother years before she was able to forgive me, because when you do not actively *practice* the skill of forgiveness, you are not able to forgive quickly. Like any other skill, if you do not practice on a regular basis, you get rusty. When you are rusty, you lose the ability to make different choices.

I practice forgiveness on a daily basis. I am committed to keeping my skill-set high. After all, I have been *blessed* with countless people I *had* to forgive at one time or another. It took me a while to believe, without any doubt, the overwhelming evidence that forgiveness is a required ingredient of true happiness. If you want inner peace and contentment, or just to grow as a person, you must master this skill. Mastering the skill of forgiveness takes you to another level of spirituality.

Whether you believe Jesus was the son of God or whether you believe Jesus did not exist, you cannot ignore the story of the biggest example of forgiveness that has ever been told. While alive, Jesus taught forgiveness. During his last hours of life, Jesus *was* forgiveness. I am sure you recognize this important quote from the Bible:

"Father, forgive them, for they know not what they do"
~ Luke 23:34

Have you ever thought about how powerful that statement really is? Can you imagine how anyone, man or woman, has the ability *in the moment*, while nailed to a cross, being tortured, mocked, and slowly and unmercifully executed, to utter those words? An act of forgiveness at such a crucial moment seems impossible to comprehend; however, without forgiveness, you have sentenced yourself to an internal prison.

How to Instantly Forgive: Since I have learned the skill of forgiveness the hard way, I have learned several facts. I have also discovered strategies that will aid you on your quest to be able to forgive anyone for anything.

Five Facts about Forgiveness: 1) You make a choice to forgive; 2) You make a choice not to forgive; 3) You cannot pick and choose which behaviors to forgive. . . ALL circumstances fall under the heading of forgiveness; 4) Forgiving is Health Food for Your Soul; and 5) Forgiving is Contagious; 6) Forgiveness does not require words. In fact, forgiveness is an actual energy that you emit.

When You Are Challenged: When you are given opportunities to forgive remember this: Whatever has happened, never take a "slight" personally. This is a really tough concept, but one that is necessary to grasp. How many times have you been angry because of how someone else drove in traffic? It is easy to get angry with someone who just cut you off in traffic; however, there is more than one way to interpret the same incident. Maybe the driver had received a phone call informing him that a loved one was just rushed to the hospital. Would you be forgiving of his driving behaviors if you knew those were the circumstances? I know I would.

Let us say your forgiveness skills are at best rusty, or at worst non-existent. There is hope. Remember, you will not be able to pick and choose your circumstances, but you will be able to choose a different behavior than what you are used to. On February 21, 2013, I was in New York City. It was my only son's twenty-eighth birthday, and while he worked I decided to visit the 9/11 Memorial. I was in awe of the surroundings. From my perspective the site exuded peace, growth, and the resilience of man. Before my eyes I witnessed the undeniable Universal Law of Cause and Effect. There is never a cause without an effect. Is it possible to forgive nineteen terrorists who brought death and destruction to thousands on that day? Only YOU can answer that question. What I do know is this: whether you chose to practice forgiveness or whether you chose not to practice forgiveness *you will be choosing* how you will somehow, someway, be immediately affected.

When you begin spending the majority of your time forgiving instead of keeping score, you will feel lighter, freer, happier, and unbelievably powerful.
~ *Rebecca L. Norrington*

Quality of Life from the *Outside:* Can you achieve Quality of Life from the outside? Let us take a look. What is missing in your life? What do you need TODAY to experience a satisfying quality of life? Are you able to list five things that are missing in your life? Ten? Twenty? More than twenty? If you have a paper and pen handy, how fast can you list all the things you would need that would qualify you for a life of quality? Would it take you a few minutes, a few hours, or a few days? When I tried this exercise, I could not write fast enough. Do not include something in your list like *world peace*. The items on your list have to be items YOU are missing to complete YOUR mission of achieving quality of life. What if I told you I was able to make everything on your list appear?

How do you *feel* listing all the things you are missing? Good? How many items did you list that if you had the money, you would be able to purchase? All? If there was even **one** item that you are able to purchase, then you are determining your quality of life from the *outside*.

The perception that there is something missing from our lives is one of the biggest reasons for unhappiness. When we think something is *missing*, we are subtracting from our quality of life. Anytime you believe something is missing, you create the vibration of being dissatisfied. When you are dissatisfied, you carry that feeling into your present and future moments. Do you _really_ want to tell the Universe you are dissatisfied with what has been given to you? The perception of not having enough _____ (fill in the blank) is what keeps us stuck on the belief that life itself is not enough.

When you focus on what is happening on the *outside*, there is a never-ending list of "things to do" and thoughts of "I'm not good enough". The good news is your perception can be changed with a snap of your fingers. Your circumstances do not have to change. Your partner does not have to change. The only thing you have to do is choose to change your way of thinking. Let us start being grateful for what **is** in every moment, and the quality of your life will improve dramatically.

Quality of Life from the Inside: *Can you achieve Quality of Life from the Inside? Let us take a look.* Can you imagine looking at your image in the mirror **knowing** the following?

"I'm completely perfect just the way I am!" (What was I thinking?)
*"There's nothing **I have to do** to be loved."*
*"There's nothing **I have to do** to be successful in the eyes of God."*
"Everything in My Life is in Divine Order."
"Everything that happens is for my betterment."

YOU are the most powerful person in the Universe! More importantly, your power is your birthright; and you do not even have to search for your power. Your power lives INSIDE of you.

Your Perspective Can Change the Quality of Your Life: CHANGING YOUR PERSPECTIVE CAN IMMEDIATELY CHANGE THE QUALITY OF YOUR LIFE. Are there thoughts that you ALWAYS think? For an example: "I need to lose weight", "I'm not doing enough", or "I'm not good enough" or _____ - you fill in the blank.

When I say, "When you change your perspective, you can immediately change the quality of your life," I am not talking about finding a new job, inheriting money, moving into a new home, finding your soul mate, or adopting a pet. All of the things I mentioned *would* change your life – but only for a brief moment in time. I am referring to permanent change, a change that will enable you to *add*, on a daily basis, to the quality of your life.

It is simple, and it will allow you to be more creative with your thoughts! Be prepared to discard the way you have ALWAYS thought. That is right; your played-out, rigid thinking can be discarded and replaced with creative thinking. Can you even imagine adopting different thoughts? If you are thinking the same thoughts today as you were thinking yesterday, then you are not growing. More importantly your results will not change. Do you agree?

I will give you an example of what I experienced recently. A co-worker was clearly upset when I saw her one morning. I have known her for a few years, and her demeanor shocked me because she is usually very calm and easy-going. She has the type of personality that does NOT make waves. When I greeted her, she was visibly upset. Of course I was curious and asked her "What's wrong?" Now, before I tell you what happened, there is a magic word contained in the first sentence. See if you can pick it out.

Her face contorted as she recounted, "I was on the freeway and I almost got into a huge car accident." (Magic word?) She was extremely angry and visibly upset while sharing the harrowing story that had happened over an hour before. As she continued with the story, I found out she was able to cleanly dodge the car accident. I was shocked. Why? Because she was reliving an event she experienced **two hours** earlier. She refused to let it go. She was so angry at the other driver that she chose to suffer for more than two hours. Admittedly, avoiding a car accident while on the freeway is pretty harrowing and stressful *in the moment*. And it is reasonable to enjoy a few minutes to recover, but two hours? I asked her, "Are you going to focus on what ***almost*** happened or are you going to focus on the fact that because you are such a great driver, *you avoided* an accident?" This is creative thinking. At that point she became angry with me because of my question. What was her priority in the moment? What would you do? You always have a choice. You have the ability to focus on what is wrong in the moment or you can focus on what is right in the moment, implementing some creative thinking.

After a few minutes of focusing on the negative aspect of any situation, guess what you begin to attract more of? What do you think my co-worker will attract as long as she holds onto this "horrible" memory? Now, she does not see anything *wrong* with the way she was processing and unloading her stress. Like I have said, we are all as different as our finger-prints. However, becoming *aware* of when and how long we hold on to negativity is the beginning of change. With change comes growth. With growth come more choices. With more choices you become open to more possibilities. With more possibilities you become more creative. When you become more creative, the quality of your life will increase. *A small shift in your perspective can change your life.*

Ask and It is Given: Questions to ask the Universe to Improve the Quality of <u>YOUR</u> Life: 1) *How* does it get better than this? 2) What else is possible? *3)* How can I contribute to the betterment of this world? 4) How can I feel JOY all day, everyday - today, tomorrow and forever? 5) *How does the Quality of LIFE get better and better and better?*

Life is a Gift: Close your eyes and think back: Can you remember being blown away by a gift you received? It does not matter who gave it to you, just think about what it was. Maybe if you are fortunate, you can think of more than one gift that left you speechless – that gift that physically caused your eyebrows to rise while your mouth fell open! You might have even jumped up and down while screaming with joy.

Can you remember how excited and happy you were? Can you remember how you felt?

I am here to announce that LIFE is a gift! In fact, the gift of LIFE is more valuable than any other gift I can think of. To be able to experience this thing we call LIFE in any form or fashion is a daily gift. It is beyond words and explanation. With every breath we take, we experience this gift of LIFE. You will wake up every morning grateful for the gift of life. You will consciously spend moments throughout your day remembering how fortunate you are to have this gift of life. You will spend more time loving and less time hating. You will spend more time forgiving and less time blaming. You will spend more time accepting and less time judging. You will spend more time opening your arms and less time pointing fingers (yes that finger). When you embrace these ideas, the quality of your life will change.

I hope what I have learned will encourage you to make some changes in your life. Everyone deserves to enjoy quality of life, but I have learned that it is our choice to decide when and how to make it happen.

Chapter 4

What Do You Dream About and What Are You Worth?

ﷺ

Contributor: Joseph J. Farina

I met Joe by accident. We were at a seminar in a room of over 500 people. We started talking and found so much common ground between us. Joe is part of my Time to Play project, helping people find the resources they need to enjoy life, and we both share the belief that there is a higher motivator guiding us in our endeavors. Dreams are just the beginning, but the most important key is to believe and have faith that ANYTHING is possible. Joe's chapter is a tremendous resource and a heartfelt account of his personal and spiritual growth.

Like Joe, I believe that the root of our problems is lack of self worth and our belief that we are not "good enough". I believe this belief is the trigger that causes us to partake in self-destructive behaviors. It is the root of our fears. It is what holds us back. My lack of self worth and my need to prove I was "good enough" was the reason for my "striving for the brass ring". Do we all have some type of lack of self worth? It is so important to recognize what triggers this in us and to begin the healing process.

I am truly grateful to Joe for sharing what he knows now. His account of his journey will certainly help others. I hope you see yourself, or a loved one, in his chapter. I hope you can find the ability to begin to awaken the amazing power within you. I advise that you do the short exercise Joe included at the end of this chapter. I believe it will help you, tremendously, as you begin your own journey to pursue your dreams.

— Daren

A man steps up to the plate. It is two outs and the bottom of the ninth. He stares down the pitcher. The fastball comes, he hits it, and out of the park it goes! A golfer sets up for his tee shot. Armed with a 3 wood he faces the final hole of the championship. He swings, and it easily lands on the green and rolls into the cup. The championship is won! The scene of the baseball player is timeless. It is a dream of a little kid acting out their greatest future moment. The scenario with the golfer is no different; some young child's dream of greatness in the years to come. These dreams are big and vivid. They burn in the child's mind where the scenes of greatness are acted out. I am sure that you can relate, on some level, with one of your own childhood memories. I had those same exact dreams as a child. However, for me I had to ask myself years later, "What happened to that dream?" Can you relate to this question?

My name is Joe Farina. I am a Motivational Speaker, Entrepreneurial Trainer and Professional Network Marketer. I would like to thank Doreen Guma for asking me to contribute to this book and offer some insight of what I have learned over the years. The title of this book will serve as the back bone for this chapter, and it is my prayer that this information can serve you in some way to improve your life! I believe that information is better received when we know a little bit more about the person delivering the message.

I grew up in a small town in Spring Mount, Pennsylvania. My father worked at a state correctional facility as a corrections officer and my mother was, and still is, one of the sweetest people I have ever known. I was an athlete, and by all accounts, in my youth a happy and motivated "big thinker". I had my whole future in front of me and I was excited. I was always a dreamer and loved a challenge. I constantly dreamed of greatness. I grew up in a time of freedom and amazing adventures. I will never forget the early years of my childhood. I cannot remember a bad time. Things drastically changed for me in my teenage years. My father became very sick and for several years I had to watch my biggest hero and role model break down and wither away. To me he was like the incredible hulk at 5 foot 10 inches and 265 pounds. My father's feats of strength are still legendary in some social circles. He embodied so much of the man I wanted to become. I remember when I was thirteen and I beat my father in an arm wrestling match. That marked something very troubling, and my father went on to spend the last year and a half of his life in a hospital. He passed when I was fifteen, and it felt like a part of me also passed. There is more to my life, but I will stick with the bullet points. What died that day with my father were MY DREAMS. It took me years and years to even come close to recapturing them. In the spirit of "*If I knew then what I know now*", I will share with you what I found to be the reasons why.

I am going to share a very powerful thought, one that if you understand, I believe will revolutionize your life. That thought is this, **what you dream about is intertwined with what you feel you are worth. Likewise, what you feel you are worth is intertwined with the size of your dream**. There was a great movie with Sylvester Stallone, it is the final movie in the Rocky storyline entitled *Rocky Balboa,* and in it Rocky says this quote:

> "*Let me tell you something you already know. The world ain't all sunshine and rainbows. It's a very mean and nasty place, and I don't care how tough you are, it will beat you to your knees and keep you there permanently if*

you let it. You, me, or nobody is gonna hit as hard as life. But it ain't about how hard you hit. It's about how hard you can get hit and keep moving forward; how much you can take and keep moving forward. That's how winning is done! Now, <u>if you know what you're worth, then go out and get what you're worth</u>. But you gotta be willing to take the hits, and not pointing fingers saying you ain't where you wanna be because of him, or her, or anybody. Cowards do that and that ain't you. You're better than that!"[2]

I love this quote and I have underlined a small part of it. *"If you know what you're worth, then go out and get what you're worth."* Rocky nailed it on that one.

I can honestly say, in retrospect, that one of the biggest things that contributed to my lack of dreaming was that I did not know what I was worth, and if I tried to establish my value, I always felt it was very little. As I look back now after years of personal development and achievements, it seems true that the size of my dream was equal to what I felt I was worth. You see, one cannot dream big when they feel so small, and for years after my father's passing I felt almost invisible.

Let us look at an example of one of the greatest dreamers of all time and see if we can measure his worth and how important he felt his message was. Can you guess who that is? It is the one and only Dr. Martin Luther King. He stood up in front of the world and said "I have a dream." I will not go any further in quoting it. If you have not read his famous speech, you should consider taking the time to do so. Dr. King came out and said point blank, with bold conviction, that he had a dream. I am not sure you can get clearer than that. I believe Dr. King was able to pursue his dream because he knew what he was WORTH. He knew what he was put on Earth for, and it was tied to his DREAM.

Many of us have struggled with doubt and fear that may have knocked us out of a game, a job, or perhaps, beat us into submission and robbed us of our purpose. If that has ever happened to you, like it has happened to me, then it may because your DREAM was not big enough and your self-worth was not there. It is a funny thing when we have to fight for something. It is a funny thing when we get pushed around because only one of two options can happen - we either rise to the occasion or we fall in defeat.

I will share with you something right here that I have found to also be true. If you have a pen or highlighter you may want to underline or highlight it: *Your willingness to go the distance is intertwined with the power and size of your dream and what you believe your worth is.* I am no different than anyone else in the sense that I am here by the grace of God and I live in the same world. However, my dream is unique to me just like your dream is unique to you.

Here is the crazy part though, and it is that if we do not feel or understand or own what we are worth, how big do you think we are going to dream? Take a moment to think about how big your dream is. Mediate on it for several minutes. See how big you can dream before your lack of worth allows for self-doubt or limiting beliefs to take hold. Try this everyday and see if, like a distance runner training to go further, how far you can go. Work your dream everyday during times of meditation. When you feel like you cannot possibly dream bigger, push it just a little further. When my father passed away and I let go of the fight, dreaming of a brighter future seemed almost wrong, and with my low sense of worth, at times, seemed too painful.

Years later that outlook changed for me. I found that dreams are a safe place and you should grow to love them as you would love yourself and those around you. The world is a better place when we allow the beauty of who we are to shine forth. The first part of that process is the dream. Enjoy it.

If you understand where I am coming from then you will understand that identifying and owning and embracing your priceless worth in this world is not only a powerful key to success, but something more. It is your duty, obligation and command to do so. It is part of your purpose to pursue your dreams and to understand the one of a kind creation that you are. It is your gift to the world when you dream HUGE and then work to share the dream.

When I am on stage as a Motivational Speaker, it becomes apparent to me all the time that I am living out one of my dreams. From that very dream springs forth a passion. That passion is to awaken the dreams of others. It had to start as MY dream before I even walked in front of a crowd. It started there because I had finally understood that I was "worth it", and from that I realized that others were "worth it" also.

I get chills when I look back on my experiences that have lead to this point. I look at my relationship with the Lord and how that has changed me. Many of you do not know me on that level, but I am proud to share with the world that my greatest moment and biggest turning point for me was accepting Jesus Christ as my personal savor. I began to read the Bible and digest the greatest wisdom for mankind. From that I have an understanding of my place in the world. I had an awakening of my dream and my sense of worth, which created the man I am today. There is power in the dream, but like I said throughout this chapter, it must come from a high level of self-worth in order to grow and thrive. It also comes from an understanding that we are not here by mere chance. *Just think about that!* I believe dreams come from a place of Faith. Let us move on, shall we?

Let us go back to looking at a dream and how powerful it can be. The power of a dream gives us the ability to keep striving everyday even though it does not look like we are going anywhere. The power of a dream and the understanding of what we are worth says, "I'm already living my dreams; I'm just telling my story of how I got there". Too often in life we stop dreaming like the little boy who wanted to be at the plate, with two outs in the bottom of the ninth, in the last game of the world series, and ready to hit the homerun to win that game. We start settling for high school glory stories because, as we move on through life, we forget what we are worth.

Another truth for me is this: **Where you are at today is a direct result of what you dreamed yesterday**. Can we change our dreams? Can we expand our thoughts? Can we establish goals to accomplish in order to attain the dream? Can we change what we feel we are worth? *The answer is YES!*

Make this note: We do not need to change what we are worth, and the reason for that is our worth is already established. **We are priceless!** What we do need to do is to change what we *feel* we are worth. You have to know that you are priceless before you can dream beyond what seems impossible to mere men who are held back by fear and lack of Faith.

When you understand what you are worth, your dreams will extend and expand beyond any dream that you have ever previously dreamed. It will begin to grow and thrive without limitations. That dream will continue to grow, and grow, and grow. You will begin to develop a culture of endless possibilities because of your priceless worth and the immense size of your dream. When this occurs, I pray that you rattle and shake the foundations of the *status quo* of this society. Do you believe that is possible for you? It seems like the answers are right in front of us. It also seems like the darkness of this world wants to oppress the dreamer, and if possible, wipe them out. Dr. King said it best when he said, "I have a dream," and it was tied to the worth of the human race. What are you worth and how big are you willing to dream?

I know that I have given you a lot to think about in a very short period of time. I also know that, as you carve out time to think or meditate on what I have covered so far, you will begin to develop a deeper understanding.

Some of you may be thinking to yourself, "Hey Joe, I don't know what to dream about. I don't even know what I want to do with my life." To that I say this, "Yes, you do. You know exactly where and what you want to be. You really do!" The problem is that, if you are like me, it was buried under many layers of junk, "garbage" thinking, prideful actions, selfish motives, and sinful thoughts. The Holy Bible talks about letting your light shine. The exact verse says,

You are the light of the world. A city set on a hill cannot be hidden ~ Matthew 5:14

What happens when we let our light shine? Well, I am here to tell you that a whole bunch of things can occur. One major point is that the light allows us to see the dreams that have been hidden in the darkness. Setting yourself on higher ground allows for you to see things differently and from a different perspective. Think about how much more you can see looking out from on top of a hill. You can see vast amounts of land. The world is much bigger. When you see the world as bigger you can, and will, dream BIGGER!

Know that you have an infinite amount of possibilities. Your dream and your worth is where it all starts. The path to building up your self-worth and cultivating your dreams can be found partially in what you are doing right here. My advice to you is simply the same advice that I learned from listening to Jim Rohn, and that is to read as many books as you can. Begin to listen to the great thinkers and dreamers of the world. Watch seminars on DVD. Get CDs of topics that you want to learn about and drive around in your car and do what Zig Ziglar talked about, make your car an automobile university. Look for live seminars coming to an area near you. Better yet, find one that you have to travel out of your comfort zone to get to. The effort alone will grow and stretch you. Start looking for any and all possible opportunities to grow personally. What I am ultimately telling you to do in order to understand your worth and begin to dream big is to do something called *personal development*.

Personal development is vital for your improvement. Personal development means to work on yourself, to learn new skills and expand your level of knowledge and become more then you were before. Look for the areas that you struggle in, and if you are not sure ask someone. They will tell you for sure. Once you identify the areas where you struggle, begin to develop skills to improve that area of your life. Over time you will begin to truly see that you are capable of learning amazing things. This process will increase your feelings of worth and in doing so expand your ability to dream.

I would like to issue a challenge to you as I wrap up this chapter: Once you have finished reading this, I would ask that you close the book for a moment and go grab a pen and a piece of paper. I would ask that you write a letter to yourself. In this letter I want you to tell yourself how important you are to the world. I also want you to tell yourself, in this letter, to fight for your dreams. Write it as if you where writing to someone else. I know it seems strange to write a letter to yourself, but trust me, it works. This letter should be encouraging, and when you read it, you should feel good.

My prayer for all of you is simply that you live a life that resembles your dreams. Remember to shine your light and be all that you can be. Live your dream and know your worth. I can only imagine what the Joe Farina from years ago would say to me today. I wonder what he would have thought about this chapter. Two different lives and two different people, but boy, I sure wish I knew then what I know now!

Chapter 5

Once Shy

୶ఞౖ

Contributor: Laura Francomano Facini

"Reality is what we take to be true. What we take to be true is what we believe. What we believe is based upon our perceptions. What we perceive depends upon what we look for. What we look for depends upon what we think. What we think depends upon what we perceive. What we perceive determines what we believe. What we believe determines what we take to be true. What we take to be true is our reality."
~ Gary Zukav

*L*aura's discussion about her experience growing up shows us how greatly what we perceive converts to what we believe. In her situation, even with her parent's support, Laura shows us that nothing anyone can say will change our perceptions. Laura's account emphasizes how it is up to each one of us to control our thoughts and change our beliefs about ourselves.

Through the stories shared throughout this book, it has been shown that something we might have identified as trivial that occurred in our past can later be identified as an underlying cause exhibited in a behavior that we may find displeasing today. In some of our stories it has been described how an event can stay with you and hold you back throughout life.

How many times has someone approached you, a boss, a parent, a friend, a spouse, a child, and asked a question that greatly affected you? Even after so many years have passed, it was hard for Laura to relive the moment that changed her. In her account, she noted that the question was trivial; but we can see how something not intended to be malicious was dramatically perceived and life altering. Laura's story is not something to take lightly. We have to realize that what we say, or our behavior towards another person, may have a profound impact on them. Many of the stories in this book show how important it is to be aware of this when communicating with others. Especially now with social media, many times things people post cannot be retracted, causing ruined reputations and irreversibly hurt feelings.

Laura and I often speak about the plight of our kids and what they face as they grow up today. I agree that the world is so different then when I grew up. Things are so much faster now-a-days, and decisions, at times, seem harder. My Time to Play team, of which Laura is a part, are acutely aware of the issues facing our youth regarding confidence and self esteem. If we all become aware and do our part to support our children at home, at school, and in the workplace, things can only get better for them. I am not only referring to our own children, but all children. Hillary Clinton said, "It takes a village to raise a child," and I cannot agree more.

I thank Laura for sharing her story. I know how hard it was for her to write about her feelings and the many years she was affected. Her story shows how she was able to trigger a shift to make her life amazing, and that there is always hope for others to do so, as well. Her story emphasizes how we all may struggle, but that it is **always** our choice how we move forward, whether in a positive or self-destructive manner.

— *Doreen*

I am moments away from my fiftieth birthday. While many of my family and friends have decided to slip unnoticed into their fifties, I will celebrate it. Life is moving as quickly as my parents had promised me it would when I got to this stage of life, so marking this milestone is that much more important for me. I still laugh today at the photo of my father's fiftieth surprise party that took place almost exactly thirty years ago in our family's Long Island back yard. I am stunned that it is already my time, but happy to know I will have a picture for my daughters to look back on.

At age fifty I am partnered with my husband Charlie of twenty-five years in a successful, long standing graphic design and software development company. For our entire married life and even a few years prior, we have been self-employed. My graphic skills, gift of gab, and desire to be a decision maker are put to use every week. It is safe to say that in my life now I am never described as shy, neither in business nor in my personal life. That was not always the case, and I will explain.

I was born in 1963 and spent my childhood living very comfortably in a pretty home in a quiet little cul-de-sac. I was very close to my brother Doug who was just a year older, and had several close neighborhood girlfriends of varying ages. With big imaginations and limitless energy we enjoyed after-school free time and endless summers together. I had a very happy and healthy relationship with my mom and dad who were involved parents, as involved as parents of the 1960s and 1970s were. I always felt loved and watched over by my oldest brother, Ken. We were five completely different people, yet as a family the dynamic was just right, and I was grateful for my family life.

Life outside of my neighborhood of close friends and family was different. I was painfully quiet and shy. I did my fair share of silent staring while people tried to engage me. I struggled with self-esteem from the first day of kindergarten all the way through my high school days. In school I preferred to blend into the background. Walking into a library or cafeteria could bring me to a point of panic. The more people sitting as I was standing or walking, the greater my anxiety. The panic did not completely engulf me, but it drew every bit of saliva out of my mouth as my heart would race.

I dreaded so many aspects of my school day. Since I was highly skilled at blending into the background, my walks through the school went unnoticed for the most part, as I had hoped. I was successful at being the girl not seen, and luckily was not on the list of kids to be picked on, and there was a list of those.

The teachers liked me and my grades were excellent. Since I was not shy around my family and friends, a reason for my awkward shyness around others came from an issue I had with my weight. I was too thin. Puberty was going to have a late onset as promised by my family's genetics, so I was "Twiggy" for a long stretch of time. Despite all the promises that puberty would bring on wonderful changes, I hated feeling different. Waiting seemed like a ridiculous solution and I resented that time was my only resolve. I did not like the way I looked so my self-esteem was low. Kids are schooled not to pick on the heavy set kids or people with disabilities. The "too skinny" thing never made it to the memo. I know that I was a relatively happy girl living in a safe and caring environment, and that my issue was relatively minor as compared to all the potential issues that I could have faced. However, my story illustrates how alert our adults have to be to address a child's emotional trials, both at home and throughout their school years, to help them grow in confidence. Self-esteem will not just be there. It develops based on our experiences and has to be nurtured. I have yet to see a profile of a child that will have low or high self-esteem.

I do not recall great efforts to control bullying when I was younger like there is today, but I do recall small efforts including short films in class, sitting red-faced in gym class watching the puberty videos, and being glued to the TV watching ABC afterschool specials that addressed some issues kids faced. I recall that self-esteem was a topic that was covered, but even with an effort in place to address self-esteem, it was just too easy to feel low, and I did. "Shy" was one of those things parents, teachers and administrators assumed you would grow out of and was not readily addressed.

And, yes. There is that one specific incident that could be called my "moment". I am embarrassed to write about it, because it is so minor on the scale of moments and traumas that people are truly burdened with and write about. But it illustrates just how small and seemingly incidental a personal moment can be. It is so easy to make an impact on another person, positive or negative, deliberate or accidental. Events and words can be powerful, even life altering.

Here it goes. . . In third grade our class was quietly waiting in single file to be lead in an orderly manner to art class. The girl behind me, whom I liked because she was always smiling and very sweet, turned to me and asked me innocently if I was so skinny because I was sick. She asked without any hesitation and I awkwardly answered her with the quietest, "No," as a rush of heat took over my body. Some of the other kids heard it, and it was at that moment that **feeling** different became **being** different. And, different was not good. I did not show it on the outside other than the uncontrollable flush in my cheeks, but internally I was horribly upset. This little girl meant no harm, but her words hurt. Her healthy kid curiosity and lack of the filter adults use to prevent themselves from getting punched in the face drove me to tears. The tears did not come, of course, until my face hit my pillow after racing home from school. What a ridiculous little moment, you would think. I am sure my mother addressed it, expecting me to forget all about it. This should not have been a life changing moment that makes for an afterschool special, but it was for me.

In a day or so, it should have faded, but it did not. How could that little girl have known that inside of my head were monumental doubts and that I was so fragile? I cannot tell you why I was so fragile, I just was. I am sure that the same comment would not have damaged a different little girl. People are complex, so complex that the simplest of statements can have a grand effect. From that moment on, my dear sweet mother spent a lot of years addressing my issue of weight and self-esteem with me over and over again, as I packaged it in so many creative ways. She tried, and I love her for that. When it was time to go shopping for back to school outfits, for example, I would tell her we should not bother because I was too skinny and ugly. So much drama from a tiny girl.

She tried, and yes, she tired of it. She eventually stopped trying and I knew she was worn out from my "oh, dear me" moments. No one in my life has ever been as level-headed and easy going as my mom. When she started pulling away that had a profound effect on me, and not in a way you would expect. She did me a tremendous favor and she never knew it. More than I hated being too skinny, I hated disappointing people, especially those people I loved and admired. Maybe because I knew how much I truly was loved it protected me from feeling hurt when my mom pulled back. Because my anxieties were causing my mom to feel bad, it became a trigger for me to change.

Throughout my youth I gravitated to adults and I spent the best hours of my childhood sitting at a dining room table enjoying the conversations of my parents, aunts and uncles. I surrounded myself with a loving support system.

Each school year began the same way. The first day of school was stressful because of all the unknowns. I had recurring nightmares that I would not find my classroom, or worse, that I lost my school schedule. I had to run through the hallways time and time again to the main office to get another schedule, invariably making me late for class, and having to walk into a room where everyone was sitting. My "Charlie Brown" cartoon-like nightmare lasted for years. But, as each year started the same, they began to end a little easier. As slow as the progress was, I was changing.

Today I am a competent, confident woman. How did I get here? Once shy, always shy is certainly not a truth for me. Did I just outgrow it as others believed I would? Were there words or moments that kept me on the right path? Could I have gone the other direction? Since everyone's journey through life is different, what was it that allowed me to gain the self esteem to be the person I am now? It may have been my mother's sad but warm side glances, my father's unrelenting desire to fix everything for his little girl, or simply puberty's "magic" that lead me to a decision that ultimately changed my life's direction.

Some more background information: I did have a few month-long boyfriends in high school, and I did make three close girlfriends in my junior year of high school. My girlfriends and I bonded thanks to very similar stories, and I appreciate them for the importance they had in my survival of my junior and senior years. Together we made it to graduation as the "quiet girls" who found it easier to relate to the teachers than to most of the other students. Our grades were outstanding and we were success stories on paper. Of these friends, one became the high school valedictorian and another the salutatorian.

Well before graduation, somewhere around the middle of my junior year, I became determined that I would go to college somewhere that required an airplane flight to get there. I knew it would be too easy to stay close to home and in the comfort zone of my cul-de-sac life. After all, my mom and dad were loving supporters and people I actually liked. I felt inside that I needed to grow and knew that home was no longer the place to do it. I was hopeful that I could build my self-esteem by going someplace where no one knew me, and starting over sounded exciting. I broke my dad's heart by choosing five schools in Florida. The little girl who feared her walk across a school cafeteria was not turning back and was making her way to a university with an undergraduate class of 30,000 plus students.

The University of Florida in Gainesville became a place for me to ignite my change. I was very excited and even more scared. My first semester at college proved to be one of the most stressful, yet memorable, times in my life. Literally, my hair was falling out of my head as I faced my everyday adventures with a great deal of anxiety. It was this very short time period which broke me out of the shell that could have kept me from the life I know now. I was finally experiencing the growth I had longed for. Having made a great transformation in confidence, in my sophomore year of college I was even able to admit to myself that I should pursue a degree in graphic design. I knew I had to leave Gainesville, a place nearly devoid of art culture in the 1980s. Everyone but me seemed to have known that design was my destiny. I let my parents know about my revelation and decision. They supported me without hesitation, and I was accepted by and transferred to the School of Visual Arts in Manhattan. What would have been my junior year in U of F became my freshman year at SVA. I returned to my cul-de-sac, the bedroom I grew up in, and began dating my high school boyfriend Charlie once again. Charlie made me feel smart, pretty and important, and our relationship was fantastic. I commuted to Manhattan to pursue a Bachelor of Fine Arts in Graphic Design. I had set myself on a clear path of personal growth and was succeeding. Being back in my familiar and safe surroundings and living, once again, with my loving parents was now a part of my positive journey. Charlie and I married in 1988 and in 1996 started a family. We are the parents of two amazing daughters, Samantha and Valerie. Now as I am about to turn fifty, they are teenagers, thirteen and sixteen years old. I am witnessing their journey through a time period that I personally found difficult, sometimes even horrifying, yet wonderful in other ways thanks to a great nuclear and extended family. Because of what junior high and high school had meant to me and the obstacles I faced being a teen, it is not difficult to imagine that I worry a great deal about the self-esteem of those I love and care for. Parents are natural worriers, yes, but I cannot help being extra concerned about them. I even worry about each and every one of their friends. I feel a tremendous amount of empathy for the teens of today, and I am scared for them.

With all the school programs and "no tolerance" pledges, peer resolution clubs, and more, today's teens remain fragile. I witness personal struggles in my own small circle in my own small New York community. As a child of the '60s, '70s and early '80s I know I faced pressures; however, my personal observation is that kids today have to manage a constant pressure to succeed in a much broader range of areas. I hope I am wrong, but I fear that fewer children will be able to "manage" their way through all of these unrelenting pressures. Parents, schools and society send out messages. We talk about our children in social settings and we are outspoken about our high expectations, despite our own concerns that the expectations may be difficult for our kids to reach. How many of these kids know that they will be able to live a happy life and achieve great things no matter who they are or where they come from? What if they do not make the varsity soccer team, first chair in the orchestra, or don't fit an Ivy League school college application profile? Do they truly understand that no matter how they started, no matter how shy they once were, they can grow into confident adults? With confidence anything can be achieved, though it is the confidence that needs to be built, first.

Our children need us to do more than what we are doing. When so much of the pressures put on these children occur behind closed doors at home, building confidence is so much harder. We as a community cannot address what we don't see. What I ask of our communities is to offer our children hope and to build their confidence. As someone who so desperately needed to be validated, I am vocal about my pride in children's "tries" and triumphs. I am the mom who sits proudly in the audience at a school play and cheers for each child on stage, not just my own. I make sure that, while watching a dance rehearsal, I smile and cheer for the whole group. I cannot tell you how many of those kids smile back at me in appreciation. They need to be seen. There is nothing as effec- as validation toward others and nothing as easy to do.

Coming from a generation that stands firmly behind the "everyone gets a trophy" and the "no one fails" scenarios during the elementary school years, it is ironic that we take a 360 degree turn and send kids the message that they have to shine in every activity and succeed in every subject. Should we be surprised that our children are so stressed? We have the right guidance because we have our own past experiences that taught us so much. With social media now a major part of a tween and teen's life, we as parents and guardians have no past experiences to draw from to know how to help them filter this bombardment of odd information. They are not just walking through a cafeteria trying to get to a seat unnoticed, they are trying to be relevant in an "instant society" where they are in plain view of the kids they like, hate, fear and barely even know on Facebook, Instagram, Twitter and others. They throw themselves daily into an eclectic circle of mixed ages, attitudes, and groups. No one can easily slip by unnoticed as I did. Social media has taken these kids away from the privacy of their home. Where I had the control of an age appropriate, 30-minute edited sitcom that had a conflict and a clear resolution (i.e. the Brady Bunch and Happy Days), they have 24/7 reality television and internet-based media minus all the editing. Could we have actually been better off as TV watchers pre-internet than kids today?

I attended a seminar for parents of high school juniors regarding the college application process. After being applauded for being one of the few that attended, the speaker painted a grim picture, posting gloomy statistics for this college-bound generation. I was cautious. A seminar of this type can be more of a self-promotion, but the sources of the statistics provided clear insight. Colleges and universities are increasingly more difficult to get into, the freshman dropout rate is alarmingly high, prospects for jobs after graduation are dismal, starting salaries are far lower than needed to recoup costs, and students will graduate with greater debt than any generation before them. This is NOT our children's fault, but they will have to suffer through it. As creative people by nature, my husband and I may struggle less than others with presenting "creative solutions" for our children as they go through the process of finding, building and loving a career. We naturally see things from many different angles. It is important to realize that there is never one road to your destiny. There is a greater need to be more creative to stand out in the job force. I believe becoming an entrepreneur and creating and controlling one's career path will likely become more common, whether by choice or by necessity. However, before we can begin to guide our children, we should never lose focus on building their self-esteem. When one has a healthy opinion of themselves they are better able to overcome challenges, or adapt to changes, throughout their lifetime.

Even if you grew up without the self-esteem issues that others may have faced, as an adult would you recognize when your own child is deep within a personal struggle, or would you just assume no intervention is needed? They will out it, right? I acknowledge that every child will go through their adolescent period differently. Because of my experience I believe every child needs to know they have the unwavering support from the adults in their life. They need to know we will listen to them without judgment so they can be heard and helped. We can let them know that, by no means, are they doomed if they are not at the same stage that some of their peers are at. It may be as simple as giving them your positive support and the acknowledgement that they are, and will be, fine. You may have some fears and concerns, what healthy parent or guardian doesn't for the children they love; but provide solutions instead of promoting fear. Listen more than lecturing. Be a positive role model.

I think back to the days of my childhood and reflect on the moments and people that have shaped me. I know I made good decisions, and I certainly made some bad ones. I had good times and bad. Since my shyness was with me from a very early age I am fairly certain that I was wired to be just that. But it was my positive environment, the love of my family and friends, the guidance from teachers that saw my potential, and each and every experience, whether big or small, positive or negative, that shaped me. I am one of the lucky ones. My road to age fifty was so much smoother and easier to travel than many others faced or will face. I am blessed. I celebrate all of life's moments and will honor my time here by honoring others. You never know whose mountain you will move when you make their walk across the cafeteria a little easier.

Chapter 6

Where Have the People Gone?

⚘

Contributor: Geena Bean

*O*ne thing that Jim and I discuss frequently is the notable decrease in verbal communication between people. It perplexes me how our own kids may prefer texting someone or logging into social media instead of picking up the telephone or being face to face to chat. A fond memory I had from when I was younger was our home phone ringing all the time. Many days our phone is silent now. Some people do not even have a landline! But there is that frequent buzz of our cell phone texts. As a girl growing up, one of my favorite things was to be on the phone till all hours with a boyfriend. I also remember my sisters and me fighting for phone time! Remember when the technology advanced and the phone company introduced call waiting and three-way calling?

I cannot say I believe that social media is all bad, as I do use it as a networking tool. I "met" Geena because of something she posted on a website, and I became interested in her background and her story. I learned she had written a fabulous book, *Come Back Dear Sun*. When we first spoke we discovered we shared the same views regarding the decrease of community. We also both believe that the decrease of our kids' going out to play is truly a loss in our society. I am proud of her initiative to bring awareness to this very important issue. I know that once people realize what has happened things can change.

I have seen a tremendous difference in my own children growing up compared to when I was younger. Many times my eighteen year old daughter just goes to a friend's and they "hang out" while they play video games, not necessarily even talking while they play. My oldest son, now twenty-one, and I recently had a conversation about the hours and hours he "wasted" playing video games instead of experiencing life. I believe you have to participate in life and not just sit inside and play games. Each day goes by so quickly and we need to take advantage of all there is to do and see.

In our family, I do not think the change in play happened overnight. It evolved, perhaps around our busy schedules. When my kids were younger they had structured sports and structured "play dates". It was not the same spontaneous "play" that my husband and I experienced in our youth when we would just go knock at a neighbor's house and "call on" them to play. Perhaps I did not feel it was safe for my kids to play outside unsupervised; after all, is it really the same world as when we were young? Perhaps I found it easier to know where they were and that they were safe after coming home from work. After work time was always busy time making dinner, doing homework, and shifting into "home" gear and chores.

Perhaps this change in our society has contributed to changing our feelings towards each other. How many people reading this know their neighbors or talk to people on their block? I will sadly admit that I do not. It is so different than when I was a child and we knew and talked to everyone on our block. We are rarely outside in our front yard unless we are driving out the driveway. I do not believe I am imagining things. I know our lack of being outside has even affected a summer tradition in our neighborhood. We have a friend John who is an ice cream man. I remember when I was young how excited we would be when we heard the bells coming. John said business is much more difficult now, as there is no one outside playing to purchase his ice cream.

Geena was kind enough to share her thoughts on this important topic. Perhaps we have just become so accustomed to our current type of life that we forgot how it used to be. Maybe we just became too busy and forgot how to slow down. Maybe with a little reminder and some awareness things can change back, in this instance, to the "good old days"

— Doreen

⌒

Picture this, a group of children, about ten or so, running around outside chasing each other up and down the block, making their way through yards, hiding behind bushes and fences, and somehow, making their way up a tree. I use the word "somehow" because kids do not really climb trees anymore, and if you encourage them to try, they look at you like you have a giant eyeball on your head. Literally. Youthful screams wale throughout the neighborhood as the sun approaches its bedtime along the horizon; parents shout at the top of their lungs for their young ones to come inside for homework and dinner, but these children just cannot seem to stop running around, so they ignore the sounds of the alarm.

By this time, in our present day, the kids would simply be summoned on their cell phones to come home. Have you ever noticed how quiet the streets are now-a-days? Or that parents do not go outside just as much as their children hesitate to want to play outdoors? We believe that there are monsters out there and we need to protect our kids; but in the same respect, are we allowing those monsters to take over our children's playgrounds simply by not wanting to poke our heads out of the window or take a walk down the block to retrieve them? We are too busy texting on our cell phones or blogging away on our laptops to take notice that the yards and playgrounds are less concentrated with people. And when we are not texting or blogging, we are calling our kids on their cellular devices instead of going to check out the scene ourselves.

When I was eleven years old, my friends and I were usually outside playing jailbreak, kickball or softball. Jailbreak was a neighborhood tradition for us when we were little. We looked forward to it. And if our parents were not inside cooking or chatting away on the phone, they were outside doing things in the yard, or sitting on a stoop, porch, or deck. It did not matter whether you lived in the city, country or suburbs. Even though I grew up in a suburban town in New Jersey with my mother and step-father, my weekends were spent in Philadelphia, Pennsylvania with my father. There was no need to be afraid of being outside because people were constantly connecting there. Whether you were a child or an adult, there was always something to do outdoors.

Did we have video games and cell phones when I was young? Of course we did. But they were not anything like the things that we have today. Do not get me wrong; I love having a cell phone and I do not even mind throwing a soccer ball around on the television screen once in a while. But do I let these parts of modern day technology run my life? No way. There is far too much beauty and language within the world and within humanity to be so involved in things that shatter our appreciation for such admiration and splendor.

As a college graduate, children's book author, caregiver and proud aunt, I have had plenty experience with trying to encourage kids to simply be kids. I have used my experience to create epic tales and story-telling time, as well as innovative playtime outside using the power of one's imagination. I have learned that once you spend time with children at a young age and explore uncharted territories and stupendous discoveries, they become involved. They want to hear more, imagine farther, and play longer. This is why I have become a children's book author. It is within this profession that I can use my children's books to connect with kids and remind them about their own creativity and imaginations. As adults we must instill these valuable gifts, which I believe are irreplaceable.

As a professional nanny I have been lucky enough to have worked with children who seemingly do not mind playing outside. They read or use their imagination to make up silly adventures and games. There have been days when I noticed a little too much time spent in the house because of the computer or video games, but the kids in my care have had the urge to play outside. Unfortunately, I have witnessed an intense gravitation toward modern day devices like video games, computers, and television based on observing their friends and experiences shared by my friends and acquaintances. Not to mention the fact that we are living in an era of the letter "I": I want it, I do not want to, I do not feel like doing homework, I do not have to. And then there is the iPod, iPad, iPhone, iTunes, etc. Are you starting to see a similarity here? I do not know about you, but I have noticed that kids do not want to do their homework because they are too busy on mom or dad's iPhones or iPads; or, if the family is financially comfortable, the kids even have one of their own. Modern day technology is slowly replacing the intelligence, commitments, and human connections that are vital for our children to grow up to be driven, successful, imaginative, and dedicated to their passions and goals in life.

When will people stop focusing so much on banning handguns and start emphasizing the importance of limiting what video games are played by our little ones? I believe children are becoming more susceptible to violence from body parts and blood constantly being splattered all over the television. Kids are using obscenities amongst their head-sets as they hunt each other down, blowing one another's brains out. These games did not exist when I was a child. Sure, we had Mario World and Sonic the Hedgehog, but the video games that exist today are so much more realistic and violent. Could a result be that these games are, somehow, making our kids a little bit more numb when it comes to proper behavioral patterns shared among their siblings and peers? I also have observed that some children have become cranky, moody and less respectful toward elders like parents and teachers.

We must stop inviting excuses and reckless decision making into our homes. We can do this simply by communicating more and by encouraging each other to become connected through conversations. When we lose human connections, we become more ignorant and less likely to want to get to know one another. And, when we do not know each other, it is easier for us to assume things that just are not true.

Have we begun to lose the proper and full respect that we deserve by not knowing how to behave and treat each other?

You might ask yourself what does this have to do with our kids not wanting to engage in playtime or activities, but I believe it has everything to do with it. We have to continue to celebrate "the child" and encourage our children to imagine, dream, play and get along. This world can only reach its potential when people live up to their own potentials. In doing so, we must recognize that modern day technology has its consequences. Those consequences have already come full circle within our homes and now outside in the same streets that we used to play and own. We must reclaim what is our right by engaging in human connections again, or else we will never succeed at reclaiming what is rightfully ours: to always be in control of our homes, our streets, and the creativity and imagination of our children.

Chapter 7

Breakup to Breakthrough

ॐ

Contributor: Heidi Krantz, OTR, CPC

A mutual friend first introduced me to Heidi, a Professional Life Coach with a specialty in divorce. I have been most impressed with her knowledge and her passion. With statistics showing that approximately 50% of first marriages, 67% of second marriages and 73% of third marriages end in divorce[3], I knew it was important to have a person like Heidi become part of my team of professionals on TimetoPlay.com.

According to these statistics, many of us may be currently going through a divorce or know someone who is, or will be, in this situation. This chapter offers us empowerment and encouragement that there is life after divorce. As Heidi shows us, you can attain happiness and fulfillment after divorce.

I truly thank Heidi for telling her story and for sharing her emotional account with us. It has been a great privilege for me to share in her journey, how she uncovered her true passion, and how she unearthed her inner strength. I hope that what Heidi shared about what she knows now will spark many journeys to find new beginnings.

— *Doreen*

You know how it feels to be in an elevator when the car lurches up and then down ever so slightly as it reaches your floor? And, consequently, how your stomach feels like it is dropping out of your body in a sort of nauseating way? That is exactly what I felt like, all the time, for the entire one year period that my marriage dissolved before my eyes, only a lot worse. I could not eat a thing, which was a highly unusual phenomenon for me, one that I was completely unfamiliar with. I shed pounds quickly, which would later work in my favor; in the meanwhile, I was extremely weak, with little strength for daily tasks. This chronic starvation, coupled with intense exhaustion from sleep disturbance, did not enhance my coping skills or my fantasy of hiding that there was anything wrong from my children.

I was in mourning for my marriage and for my family as I knew it. I was terrified for myself and for my children and unable to consider taking any steps to move forward. Some of this may sound humorous in retrospect, but the only thought that could bring me any comfort was, "Look on the bright side, maybe the world will come to an end soon." The way I saw it, my entire universe had crumbled. My therapist asked me, "What do you want out of life in the future?" The only reply that I could muster was "I don't want to be divorced." She told me that was not an answer, but my mind was blank. I had been with my former husband from the time I was seventeen years old and then married to him for twenty years. I did not know any other "me" besides the woman who was attached to him and our three children. I was so entrenched in that identity that I had never even considered an alternative one.

The pain I endured was constant and palpable, but the way my heart broke for my children was unbearable. I knew how my divorce would potentially be harshly and deeply detrimental to each of them. At the time, my oldest daughter was seventeen years old and at the threshold of the enormous life transition of beginning college. My son was at the vulnerable age of fourteen, not accustomed to expressing his feelings and in the center of all the typical teenage challenges. My youngest daughter was only ten years old and dealing with the intense daily difficulties of being physically challenged from birth. All three were firmly attached to their identity of the "good family", intact, together, including the whole nine yards of family vacations in the tropics, family dinners at community restaurants, and holidays at home around the dining room table. Whether mom and dad were happy or not was not a concern to them, but rather a given. This was life as they knew it, a secure backdrop to deal with all the other trials and tribulations of the world, not to be fathomed as the enormous problem in and of itself.

I am embarrassed to admit that I had no connection to our finances whatsoever, and had completely surrendered control of that area to my former husband. I barely ever even wrote a check. For driving trips which were beyond local I was always in the passenger seat, believing that my ex had some magical navigation powers that I could never hope to attain. I rarely went out without my husband in the evening, with the uncommon exception of community women's events. The thought of going out for any other reason never occurred to me, as my place was always at home with my family. Even if my former husband was out at work, I perceived my role only as "holding down the fort" at home.

I had been a dedicated and devoted wife and mother with every fiber of my being for twenty years, and now I was on a roller coaster speeding down an intensely steep drop. People in my life tried to be supportive, but mostly they just looked like a blur to me with no meaning. "You're gonna be OK, you'll see," they told me. That stirred up vague feelings of anger within me. "Oh sure, like YOU know, you're going home to your husband, but I'M gonna be OK, yeah right," is what would run through my mind with no comfort felt at all. Others would look at me with pity in their eyes, put their arms around my shoulders ever so carefully and ask in a slightly condescending tone, like I had a contagious disease, "How are you doing, honey?" Well, if that did not make me feel like I was dying, I do not know what would.

Some family and close friends really did help me survive, as I could truly open up and express my all-encompassing anguish and suffering. They reminded me of my strengths, my impressive accomplishments, and how I was loved. I knew that they genuinely cared and would do anything for me. I do not think I could have lived through my divorce without my sisters. Unfortunately for me, I took on an oath of secrecy with regard to my parents, as my father was rapidly dying of lung cancer, and I just could not bear to lay this on them. I would dry my tears before entering his hospital room, so that they would not detect that anything was wrong, and then I would start to cry again when I saw my precious father suffering and my mother watching helplessly as their life as she knew it, along with her husband, disintegrated before her eyes.

Simultaneously, a close friend of mine was dying of cancer at home in her bed, and I would often go from visiting my dad to visiting her. The way that she deteriorated still haunts me, and the desperate pain of her children was more than I could bear. Sometimes, as I was leaving her home, I would have a message on my phone from my former husband asking when we were going to tell the children that we were splitting and suggesting that very same evening. I felt a crushing weight on my shoulders that I did not know how I would continue to carry. During my father's funeral and the mourning period which followed, I had a terrible nervous pit in my stomach about when I would have to shatter my children's world by telling them the news of my divorce. When would my mother be strong enough to handle this, I could not begin to imagine.

As my family worked to recuperate from the loss of our beloved father and grandfather, a few months passed. My three children left for sleep away camp, still not having been told of the impending doom. Having my children safely tucked away and enjoying themselves allowed me to begin to voluntarily relinquish my role as the "marriage saver", at least temporarily. I needed a break from scrutinizing what had gone wrong and what was continuing to head downhill, as well as from trying to revive a dead relationship. I was ready to make an independent decision that was different from what I had ever done before. I began to make plans that would focus on me.

I headed off to a three day spa getaway with a girlfriend. It was there that I began to unearth the woman inside me who had strengths and interests, and even a smile, which were separate and apart from any man. Something had begun to come together for me. Getting some distance from the toxicity of a crumbling marriage provided effective medicine for the journey ahead of me. I hiked and canoed with strangers who were happy to chat and get to know me. I joined many activities and classes on my own and connected easily with others. My tears had temporarily dried up. A voice inside of me told me that I was going to survive and that, maybe, there was a ray of hope that I could somehow even find some happiness within myself.

When I arrived home, smoothed, buffed, scrubbed, exfoliated, and somewhat exhausted, there was a lawyer's letter waiting for me in my pile of mail. My husband had officially filed for divorce. The worst and the best were ahead for me. I knew I needed to be strong and resourceful. The Universe had sent me the letter at the exact right time that I could handle it. I had just begun to discover myself and to tap into resources of resilience that I had not known existed within me.

I retained an attorney that evening, and I became a detective in terms of my finances. I hunted down and photo copied every shred of paper pertaining to our monetary history and organized all the documents into categories and files with an intensity that surprised me. However, I was not always that focused and energetic; there were days that I felt overwhelmed with the legal process and reverted to clinging to my bed with the covers over my head. There were times when I was again gripped by terror and grief and I would cry endlessly. But, in general, believe it or not, I felt I had already reached rock bottom and was on the rise. I was slowly gaining speed and strength for an uphill battle. Although the journey was sometimes jagged where I took one step forward and two steps back, I continuously moved ahead.

My home was no longer a toxic place to dread. It became my sanctuary where I was the queen of the castle. I was like a child opening her eyes after a nightmare. What I had feared had happened. My husband was gone, but I had survived. Over the next few weeks, I remember repeatedly saying to myself, "You know, this ain't half bad, this being alone thing." I began to revel in the idea that I could make my own choices without the worry of being blamed or disapproved of. I could even eat Ring Dings for dinner. The greatest gift that had happened for me was that the door to my marriage had been firmly shut with no further possibility of reconciliation. This fact of life actually gave me my wings to fly. All the energy that I had been focusing on reviving what was dead could now be refocused on reinventing my life. The seeds had been planted for future positive events that I could have never imagined would ever be part of my journey and my self-discovery.

The day that I dreaded most in my life arrived when my children returned from sleep-away camp. This was the day that we would lower the boom on them which would change them forever. Their family would be irreparably broken and there was not a damn thing they could do about it. They learned that, on certain designated nights, they would be forced to leave their beloved home and the comforts of their rooms that they were so attached to and sleep in a strange new place without me, their mom, who had always been there. They would never experience new cherished family vacations and holidays again. Perhaps they would bear a certain shame about the situation. Perhaps they would never really understand why this happened or why their parents would do this to them. I would never wish the anguish of that night we told them on anyone. I long to erase the memory from my heart, but it will always endure. This was only the beginning of the grieving, mourning and adjustment for them. Thankfully I could support them, as I was already on my way to recovery, and I would rise to the occasion. There is nothing that I would not have done or would not do for my treasured babies.

The ensuing legal divorce battle was grueling, complete with court appearances and depositions which were emotionally draining and often made me physically sick. But amidst the horror, my strength, confidence, and happiness were beginning to take root. I was learning to relate to my former husband in a brand new way with greater assertion and an ability to hold my boundaries. Something profound was happening to this forty year old woman: I was finally becoming ME.

We were living as a divorced couple during the long months of the legal negotiations. I began to think about the future that I wanted to create without considering any other adult. I found that my long career as an Occupational Therapist (OT) had gone stale and I tried a new setting in an effort to revive it. I took temporary positions in nursing homes as vacation coverage for other OTs. Although there were positives, I became aware that I now lacked passion in my work and no longer felt as if it was what I was meant to be doing. I could not envision myself ten years down the road working as an OT. I knew that I had to explore other options.

There was a new smile on my lips and a spring in my step as I thrived in the climate of possibilities. My friends and family noticed it and were impressed with my strength and resilience. They began to confidentially call upon me to encourage those in their lives who were in the raw and painful stages of marital demise. I would talk with their friends, sisters, and relatives and I would encourage them. I regularly met with success and felt enormously gratified. I wanted more and more of this connection where I could help others get through their divorce. I felt tremendous passion around it. Those who had contacted me would call me back and say things like, "I don't know what you did with my friend, but she got out of bed and went back to work," and "I don't know what you said to my sister, but she finally started her legal paperwork for her attorney." Their words helped me reach clarity on the direction of my career change. I tenaciously combed the internet for the work that would most closely match what I had been doing with these women.

This search led me to my investigation of certified life coaching programs. Studying to be a Professional Life Coach empowered me to help others with the perfect blend of emotional and practical support. The program emphasized a focus that was so exciting to me, and I learned how to help people move step by step into the future using goal oriented action plans. I realized that I had discovered how to use my natural thinking process in my new career. Just as I had taken daunting long term goals and broken them down into short term goals as an OT to reach a patient's physical objectives, I would now use this same method as a coach to approach the changes that people desired in various aspects of their lives. My OT experience would greatly enhance my coaching skills. The decision to enroll in the coaching program was mine alone and I found it thrilling. I would never have had the courage or creativity to consider this venture during my marriage. At this stage I had less money than ever before, yet I had greater financial freedom to pay the tuition. I no longer needed anybody's approval or consent in my life decisions. I was going to make this happen!

Studying Life Coaching was one of the most enormous growth experiences of my life. In order to become a coach I needed to look closely at myself, identify my own goals in various categories of my life, and then create a plan to make them happen and implement the action. I needed to discover what was blocking me from moving forward and why. While coaching others I learned to look at them without judgment and to completely subscribe to their agenda rather than my own. I mastered a way to express my curiosity in a respectful and stimulating way through the art of asking empowering questions. I learned to celebrate the successes of others with a renewed joy and excitement. I was on an emotional journey that was both healing and invigorating.

How did I accomplish all of these milestones? Besides working with the most phenomenal instructors possible and an incredible curriculum, it was through the relationships that

I cultivated with my fellow students. We coached each other through every step of the way, whether we were struggling with our fear of failure when the work seemed insurmountable, or when we were challenged with difficult emotional discoveries. We made each other feel safe and supported. Some of these relationships are among my most cherished to this day.

Earning my certification as a Professional Life Coach was exceedingly joyous to me. I approached my new career with determination, tenacity, and love. I was completely focused on growing my new business and reaching as many people going through the challenges of divorce as I possibly could. This process was and still is one of the most gratifying of my life. I became an entrepreneur, something I would never have dreamed of during my marriage. Again, I could try and even fail at various attempts, with no one to answer to but myself. I shed my fears layer by layer. My company Reinvention Life Coaching was born and I had given birth to it.

I pushed myself out of my comfort zone, got up in front of audiences, and tackled the dreaded task, the one that people rate their fear of higher than death, public speaking. Not only did I have to "pound the pavement" to get these "gigs", I had to write my own material and deliver it in an inspiring way. After many late nights typing feverishly at my computer, revising and redoing far into the wee hours and practicing relentlessly in front of the mirror, I began to make a name for myself as a motivational speaker concerning "moving-on" topics. How did this happen? It happened because I had finally found my calling. When I am up there in front of a group, I am in the zone. I am where I am supposed to be, doing what I am meant to be doing. I am connecting with people in a way that I had never experienced before. When I sense their energy shift from hopeless to hopeful, even ever so slightly, it is no different than if I scored a touchdown as an NFL player. It works because I truly believe in the message that I am delivering and find tremendous meaning in sharing it with my workshop and seminar participants. My presentations are never pure lectures. They always involve sharing from the group and exercises where people can work and practice to make the message their own. As much as I give, I am honored to learn and gain inspiration from my participants.

Business networking is another factor that helped to launch my practice. I learned to talk about my strengths and what I had to offer in a comfortable and confident way to all types of professionals. More importantly, I learned to listen to what other's work was about and how I could be helpful to them. I enjoyed this interaction immensely and I continue to love this aspect of my work. I meet countless interesting people who teach me and share so much with me. I am proud of how much I have grown and feel "like a big girl" now.

Along with growing my own business came the expansion of my technological repertoire. This is an area that does not seem to come naturally to me, but I continue to push myself to learn and master what I need to in order to reach people. I would, and still continue to, persevere for hours to accomplish what I think others might do much more rapidly. I am amazed by how far I have come in this area as evidenced by my website which I created independently using a template. It required what seemed like several hundred long tech calls for support, but my website was born along with my company and continues to be revised and updated only by me.

My work brought the opportunity for me to revive my love of writing from my very early days. I am always busy writing material for workshops, blogging, and writing promotional material. Writing is a gift that I cherish, a crucial part of who I am. I wonder what I was doing without this method of expression for all those years. Like public speaking, it is what I am meant to do.

The combination of my business networking, writing, and technological skills have all led me to my cherished clients. From my very first to my most recent, I feel honored and privileged that they chose me to share their inner worlds and the intimate details of their lives. This information is sacred, and I feel like the most fortunate person on earth to be part of empowering them to move forward and to create the lives that they desire and deserve. I cannot imagine a more stimulating and rewarding career. My spirit soars as I discover the endless goodness in each woman and man that I work with. As they push out of their comfort zones and grow, no matter how challenging that journey is, I know again that I am doing what I came to this earth to do.

The lessons I learned through my own experience fueled the niche that I eventually developed within my "moving-on" coaching: successful dating. At this time in my life I had not been on a date in more than twenty years and had little experience before that. I had to re-navigate the entire dating world, which is exactly what I now coach many of my clients to do. I had to shift from thinking I could or would never be with another man after my former husband, to having the motivation and the courage to meet and interact with strangers of the opposite sex. Well, here is where my previous months of starvation paid off. . .

As my tears dried and my "this ain't half bad" philosophy took root, I began to notice that I was being noticed. I laughed to myself and surprisingly started to become interested in what was happening around me. I had been in a dead marriage for a long time, and something inside me began to feel alive again, quicker than I would have imagined. I began to date and I took to it quite naturally. Before I knew it, my sister somehow convinced me to try online dating. She had been involved with this type of socializing for a while, and my previous reaction had been, "Yea right, I'm gonna to talk to strange men on the computer and then go meet them in person. I don't think so, not me." Flash! She was photographing me and up went my first profile onto the dating site. My writing skills came through as I wrote an engaging narrative to accompany my photo for my profile, and then my life changed. The attention that I received was truly exhilarating, and it was just the medicine that I needed after the beating my self-esteem had taken during the demise of my marriage. Yes, I did take a few emotional lumps and bumps in the dating world, which cannot be avoided, but mostly it was a lot of fun. Meeting various men, learning about them, communicating about myself, and being received enthusiastically was a totally enriching experience. Although I found it difficult to find a true connection, this phase of my journey was crucial to my healing process.

As a by-product of dating, I learned that I could drive wherever I needed to be. It was OK if I got lost, I would eventually find my way. I had no restrictions on where to go. I was in the driver's seat. This tremendous newfound freedom built my self-confidence. I did not need my ex-husband to navigate. I had a brand new husband, my GPS!

Through my dating experience I learned what I was looking for in a man. I was blessed when Steve, my true soul mate, eventually appeared on my computer screen and contacted me. Our first date was a huge success and the connection was palpable. Our conversation ran the complete gamut from laughing and joking to discussing death, religion, and parenting. The relationship grew and blossomed. Within the net of safety that Steve provided I was able to continue to grow as an individual and also to continue to heal. I learned to communicate in complex new ways, and we were able to work through whatever challenges developed between us.

Over the years, we explored so many various experiences together, from snorkeling, to skiing with our children, to the spiritual path of *Kabbalah,* to the psychotherapy model of

"Internal Family Systems". I know now that God had intervened. All my suffering had a purpose. I was introduced to a kind of love that I had never dreamed possible. You see, I had never been with an angel before. That is the most effective way that I can describe Steve's aura of light, inner beauty, integrity, brilliance, and the safety that he projects.

It was clear to me that Steve appreciated and celebrated all of my strengths and accepted and supported the entire "me" in a way that I had never experienced before. We enjoyed a mutual high level of respect and laughter that brought out the absolute best in me. I knew how highly my opinions were valued and the feeling was completely reciprocated. This connection caused me to enjoy expressing my love completely and openly. I was totally free to be myself. What an irony. What I found here I never would have imagined was possible while I clung desperately to my previous marriage a few years prior.

Fast forward, Steve and I are happily married. We recently celebrated our second anniversary. I am constantly grateful for what we have and am aware of how extraordinary it is. Our relationship fuels my passion out there every day, encouraging people that new love is possible, and that they too can find it, cultivate it, and cherish it.

Creating a blended family has its significant challenges, but it can also be incredibly enriching. We have gone through various phases of navigating the situation and taking into account everyone's complex needs. Two of my children are now married to wonderful people and I feel that my relationship with all my children has deepened and become richer since my divorce. They are all the lights of my life. Each of my children worked through their own individual complicated journey through the pain of the divorce. Although I wish I could have spared them, they each came out stronger, and in some ways happier, than ever before. Regardless of the suffering that I endured through the dissolution of my marriage, I am forever grateful for my amazing children and their spouses. I would not have traded that for anything. I have a wonderful relationship with my husband's children as well, and we truly enjoy being together.

If I had known way back then what I know now: I would have realized that many of my fears were catastrophic projections that did not come true. Thankfully, I did not disintegrate, nor did I shrivel up and die from the pain. I did not spend the rest of my life alone and lonely. I did not become destitute and homeless. I did not spend the rest of my days mourning and grieving for what was lost. I did not spend the remainder of my time beating myself up with regrets. My children made it through.

**If only I could have known then how
I would eventually reinvent my life.**

In closing, here is my message which carries some Kabbalistic inspiration: Within the pain and challenge of divorce, there is amazing opportunity to be revealed which would never have otherwise presented itself. It is up to you to find it, but please know that it is definitely there. I have shared with you some of the incredible opportunities that were born out of my intense pain. Even writing this book chapter was one of them.

Now it is time for you to write your story. Move yourself from breakup to breakthrough! Break out of your comfort zone. Discover yourself. Get in the driver's seat. Your possibilities are limitless. Make it happen.

Chapter 8

What I Have Learned After Many Years of Marriage

~❧~

Contributor: Madeline Brady

I met Maddy in 2002. She is such a giving person. For the years we worked together and now when we talk, she always helps me rationalize ideas that I come up with to put things in perspective. She is definitely one of the brightest people I know, and she freely jokes that it comes from age and learning along the way.

In 2004, when I came up with the need to write *If I Knew Then What I Know Now,* Madeline was standing right there next to me. I automatically assigned her mom the chapter for marriage longevity. Her parents, at that time, were married almost 70 years and so happy and devoted to each other. We lost Maddy's mom a few years ago, as it did take 9 years to start this book. I asked Maddy to share her mom's words of wisdom that certainly were passed down to her as reflected in her own successful marriage.

No matter how much time passes when we talk, I always consider Maddy a great friend and confidant. I hope what she has learned can be a help to you in your relationships and your marriage. As my husband and I approach our twenty-fifth year in marriage, I reflect on what Maddy has written and agree with her discussion. Make your significant other an important part of your life. I appreciate how my husband has always included me in his activities, something that has surprised many people over the years. He has told me about those who have made comments like, "You brought your wife?" And, to my reaction as to why a person would ask such a question he always tells me, "Of course I brought you. You're my best friend, and I like to be with you."

There are many times I hear people joke about how they left their spouse home. Yes, maybe people in relationships need "alone" time, but perhaps couples need to go back and look at why they got together in the first place. What drew you together? What are your common interests? What are your passions? I know I am incredibly lucky to have found someone as amazing as Jim, but if you look again at your partner, I am sure you can find that spark – even if it is deep down inside.

I have also learned after being together for all these years that you cannot rely solely on another person to make you happy. You have to find happiness inside first, and then you can be happy with another. They cannot make you happy or fill a void. Patience and consideration for others is also very important. Thinking about how the other person will feel based on your actions: if you are late and do not call, if you do not do something you have promised, etc. . . Ever hear this?

Do to others as you would have them do to you.
~ Luke 6:31

Pretty much sums it up. This may be something to keep in mind in your marriage, in your workplace, with your kids, while food shopping. . . something so simple that, perhaps, we forget to implement in our sometimes too busy lives.

I hope you enjoy Maddy's reflection and that it may get you started in strengthening your relationships.

— *Doner*

Whenever the subject of marriage arises, my husband and I are always asked if we have a secret recipe for a long and successful marriage (to each other). Almost in unison we both reply, "A great sense of humor." My husband will always quip, "Separate checking accounts." As you can see, we do not see eye-to-eye about some things, and while that is quite common, let us just say that compromise is key to marital bliss.

My husband and I have been married for 47 years and you can be certain that by this time, we have weathered quite a number of ups and downs. The highs have been extraordinary, but you can be certain that the lows have been heart wrenching. We have learned that there are no tricks and no shortcuts in a relationship. Marriage requires hard work and a deep sense of caring for one another. However, the decision to throw in the towel when you think you have had just about enough of something is often overwhelming. Rather than separating, both parties must take a long introspective look at their own actions to determine what lead to the disaster. One might say that it is like going to confession, but the penance is greater than a bunch of Our Father's uttered before you leave the church. Soul searching is a necessity in making any changes in how one deals with their partner. The challenge is for both parties to examine the issues and determine how each might have contributed to the situation.

You can pick up any magazine at the supermarket and find a "celebrities reveal their recipe on how to they keep their marriage alive" article, and yes, often you will find some solid marital advice. But it is just that, advice. Or, you may hear from an expert like Doctor Phil who usually gets an opportunity to weigh in on how to achieve marital bliss, but we later learn that he has not really achieved it either. The only way, or challenge, is to get both parties to face the issues.

We are a society that expects instant gratification, and most of us have unrealistic expectations about where life will take us. Most of us have trouble accepting the varied disappointments that come our way. Let us face it, disappointment is a constant in life and marriage plays a huge part in our daily happiness. The stress of feeling uncertain about a spouse's wellbeing can ruin the cohesive mood of a household. Therefore, it is equally important to lighten up when things go amiss. Additionally, the pull of daily obligations to kids, your job or parents often overshadow the feelings a couple has for one another. It requires a mind free of frustration and guilt about unaccomplished duties to others to ease the stress between a couple.

My parents were married for 73 years. They had eight children and provided us with a loving home. They lived in a time when there was much poverty, war and very hard work. These two wonderful and uncomplicated individuals left their country to come to America during the war. They overcame some extremely major obstacles, including leaving everything they knew behind and moving to a country that required learning a new language. They faced sickness and financial issues, but they remained faithful and devoted to one another and their family. They never wavered in their devotion to one another. I am sure that, with a brood of eight children, they were sometimes overwhelmed by their tremendous responsibility. However, they needed to get past any difficulties with each other because they had others who relied on them. Regardless of the issues, they had a deep commitment to one another. My mother's recipe for a good marriage was "*always stick together*," meaning, quite simply, that as a family unit you can overcome tremendous odds, but alone, the world can be sad and difficult. Whenever there was crisis in our home, my parents presented themselves as a united front and supported each other with respect, never using profanity to express their thoughts. They instilled in us the same values about how to treat each other and our extended families and friends, and especially how we need to treat each other in a marriage.

The question then is quite simply, what motivates couples to stay true to each other when the difficulties become overwhelming? Is it truly "love"? It seems too simple an answer to such a complex situation. Is it truly for the children that couples stay together, or is it that a separation is just too final? While it is not easy trying to rekindle a dying romance, couples owe it to each other to search for a real solution, not just take the easy way out and find someone else to make them happy. After all, once the wild fling of a new romance ebbs, marriage is much the same for most couples. A new partner may add a new dynamic at the start, but all the old baggage comes into the new relationship with the individual, and problems inevitably find a way into that marriage, as well. That is not to say that couples should stay together only out of a duty to one another, but to truly take on some of the blame when things go wrong.

I believe the most important aspect of marriage is to truly believe in each other. As life moves on in a marriage individuals may grow in separate ways. One may take a challenging job while the other may further his or her education. The stress of these new factors often leaves the other partner a bit envious that something has taken their place, leaving a void in their own lives. Perhaps a couple is dealing with children who always seem to take them in different directions with sports or activities becoming the focus of a household. Life's focus changes to supporting the kids in their challenges with nothing more important than helping them seeking that scholarship or getting into the best colleges. This is often when a couple is too busy for one another. It is at these times that it is extremely important to listen to each other as it is quite easy to miss the cues of one or the other feeling left out.

So, with all of these distractions from one another, how does a couple come back together again? There are many activities that might help including vacations together or involvement with the same sport or group activity. Most often doing just about anything together helps join a couple and enable them to grow together. Learn about the other's passions and capture the excitement of their personal interests, be that sports, science, politics or reading the same book, or simply enjoying dinner and a movie. Absorbing an enthusiasm for a new subject awakens one to the vastness of topics we are not aware of. Not only does this provide closeness between the couple, but it lends a sense of intimacy with one another. Sex is not the only activity that provides a deep sense of closeness, but it is certainly another aspect of marriage that keeps a couple close.

The expression "Live, Laugh, Love" comes to mind when I think about happy couples, but in the end I believe that Aretha Franklin said it best with her best selling recording,

"R E S P E C T". I think having respect for each other just about covers it all! It is a major characteristic in all of life. I challenge you to remember to respect each other, always.

Along the way I met Dr. Matthew Gelber, a psychotherapist with a general practice who sees many couples with marital concerns. We have had many discussions together regarding marriage longevity and what he has found that strengthens a marriage. Dr. Gelber has a lot of experience in what works in keeping a marriage together. We have talked about those who have come to his practice that had given up way too soon, how people have a fairytale vision of marriage with the great ceremony and all the stuff leading up to the wedding and then reality settles in, or those who have had life happen and forgot how to be a couple.

I asked Dr. Gelber to write a short section about what he believes makes a strong marriage, and hope what he has shared proves helpful to you.

— *Doreen*

Chapter 8 After Note

Life and Marriage

ॐ

Contributor: Matthew Gelber, MS, MFT

*C*lients always say to me, "You must have the perfect marriage." My answer is, "No, I do not, no one does." Marriage is constant care and upkeep like the rest of life. Good marriages do not just fall into place, you have to work with your partner and make it what you want it to be. With the divorce rate close to 62% it is evident a lot of people do not work at it. Without that effort, unhappiness sometimes sets in, and then, without help, a marriage can fail.

So how do you make a marriage a great one? That is the million dollar question. For me, I can apply what I have learned through education and experience with clients, but what really helps the most is what I have learned in my own marriage — teamwork, listening, understanding, respect, trust and love are some words that come to mind. I believe in returning to a belief system where communication is key. Many people have lost that in recent years. We are all disconnected and cut off from interaction in real life. Yes, we are more connected through media, but in homes we seem more disconnected and leading our own lives. I see more and more couples living as married roommates rather than in a true romance that leads to a long term marriage.

What can we do? Open up your hearts, but open up your ears even more. **Listen!** Listen to your spouse, ask questions: How do you feel? What makes you happy? What can we do to make things better? How can I help? My question to you is do you hear these questions in your home? If so, you are doing well. If not, you need to start asking.

Let us get reconnected to each other. Not only do we deserve to, but we owe it to marriage itself because that is what it is all about. We do not get married to get divorced, but if you look at the rate of return, would you invest in marriage if you saw this as a stock or a business? My answer would be no.

Imagine how good your marriage can be once you figure out the key, which is getting motivated to make it better. Make your marriage the one people aspire their own marriage to be, to admire and to enjoy to see. Get into your marriage just as you would get into your work, your family or your drive for life; make it the most important thing you do. Put down your iPod, cell phone and lap top and get in there and talk. Ask questions and make loving your partner the story of your life. We all know that couple who has been together for years and make even the hardest times in their lives something they get through together. Make love your passion and your marriage your pride.

I have learned a lot in my career, but the one thing that is always in the front of my mind is that love and care in your life is what makes you happy, less stressed, and live longer. Having a true partner to enjoy the amazing times in life and to help each other through the tough times is the ultimate. If you begin to have a mindset like this, it is not work anymore, it is love. . . . . a true love that will last forever.

Chapter 9

Always Striving for the "Brass Ring"

჻

I was born in the 1960's, a child with a stay-at-home mom and a father who was "always working" and never around. I am a research junkie and have always had a passion for finding the cause for any occurrence. Based on what I have been learning today, as it relates to my life, I understand and realize that my parents did the best they could bringing me up under the circumstances they were faced with.

In my chapter, *Digging Deeper*, I do not criticize my parents for their actions or their efforts, but attempt to show how my life evolved based on my own experience. In my life, I know things were never easy for my parents. I fully appreciate the sacrifices they have made. This chapter is an overview to show cause and effect. Combined with *Digging Deeper*, I hope that you will be able to identify something in your childhood that you have to UNLEARN, a process, forty-seven years later, which I am still working on.

In looking back, I believe that the things I observed, or experienced, while growing up caused my behaviors and feelings. It is my wish that you can identify the impressions you have formed about yourself that cause an undesirable behavior you partake in, or to recognize undesirable feelings that you have now. We all know right from wrong. We all know if we are living in a way that is pleasing or displeasing to us. I truly believe that we all have an ability to change the things we do not like, but so many of us fall into a rut and feel hopeless or helpless and do not know how to climb back out.

In my case, I did not realize I was having an undesirable experience. I think a lot of us are blind to identify that our current way of thinking or life situation is displeasing. Maybe we choose to ignore it. Maybe we do not think we can change something to make it better. Maybe we do not think we deserve to have a better, more enjoyable life. It is my opinion that, if we plant a seed in ourselves or others, it can grow and enable change. Seeing yourself in another's experience may initiate a beginning to change.

That is how Time to Play started, from just a seed of an idea based on something I observed. I started Time to Play because I was tired of seeing the sick and sad and decided to start a movement for us to take our lives back — for me to take my life back. For us to pursue quality of life, not just for us to exist in life. My husband really hates when I say, "I have seen the sick and sad," but I believe I have. I have worked in healthcare since 1987. I have had the opportunity to experience things, not as hands on clinical staff, but I have seen things that have affected me, nonetheless, including avoidable illness and avoidable suffering. Jim is a retired police officer. He has seen what I consider the bad and worse. My hope is that we can catch life situations that may affect us, in a proactive manner, before they get to the level of "bad or worse" and the police need to get involved. My goal is to help people recognize their potential and their ability to enjoy life, to see beauty in the word, and to see endless possibilities of who they can become.This common expression really sums it up:

Children Learn What They Live ~ Unknown

Again, I cannot say I had a bad childhood or a bad life. I am sure people would rather have traded in their lives for mine; however, I have identified that my <u>perceptions</u> about my experience, and what I have spent the past years choosing to believe, caused my behaviors and actions. I know now that if I had identified them sooner, my level of happiness and self acceptance would have benefitted enormously. As previously discussed, I have identified that in some way, shape or form, many of us are tortured souls, not because we have to be, but because we choose to ALLOW it to happen in one way or another.

Through talking to others and my observations, the theme of self worth and confidence continuously surfaces. In my situation, I have identified that I lived with a need to PROVE something to someone else to make myself feel good. To make me feel proud and worthy. To make me feel important. To make me visible instead of invisible. Is this the norm? Is this why people join gangs, bully others or partake in self destructive behavior? Is this the motivator for us to strive to achieve in our lives or is this a detriment? Could the solution be so simple? I believe it is. And, I believe it is something people who have lived before us identified long ago. Many authors have discussed the ills of our society and the dangers of negative self thought, but their teachings remain hidden to many who struggle along. I believe teaching self worth and confidence should be mandatory and a priority in our learning when we are young and impressionable. This thinking could change our beliefs about ourselves, empower us, and change our lives. My mission is clear. No one should feel they are unworthy. Not at three years old, ten, twenty, fifty or seventy years old. Living in self doubt is not a way to live. Think about it. If we learn to be internally healthy, strong, and confident, perhaps there would be a shift in what ails our society.

In my case, I will even go so far as to say that not having beliefs of self worth and confidence caused my actions and my need to be visible. I recognize now that I have lived my whole life trying to <u>PROVE</u> I was good enough. Guess what? No matter what I achieved, no matter what I completed, or the actions that I performed, I still remained unrecognized and unfulfilled in <u>my</u> mind and in <u>my</u> heart.

Ever hear of striving for the "brass ring"? It was an expression that came about from riding a carousel. A rider would reach for the brass ring as they rode to win a prize. This is the perfect analogy for how I have lived my life. In my situation, the proverbial "brass ring" I chose to pursue, work and strive for was the ability to say "I made it". And, guess what? I have realized I was not even proving that "I made it" to myself. However, I now recognize that, in doing so, I missed precious moments in my life that I cannot get back.

These are pretty strong realizations, right? But I feel grateful that it only took me this many years to identify it, and that I did not end my life with a belief that I somehow had failed. I have seen people who are much older than me still partaking in self destructive behavior. Still allowing their minds to control their actions. Still listening to the little voice in their head that tells them they cannot be or do something, cannot make their life better, cannot find love, cannot have money, and cannot be happy. Until they become "good enough" in their minds and in their hearts, they will remain unfulfilled.

In my career I have been fortunate enough to work in quality improvement. This means identification of a deficiency or something that is lacking and looking for ways to improve it, to search for the root cause, the "why" something has happened or is the way it is. This may be mistaken as negative thinking, but it is far from that. My intention is to identify something displeasing and then identify options for improvement that could be easily implemented. I realize that I have spent years in my personal life making **mountains out of molehills**. What does this mean? I had a problem, something I was facing, a disagreement, something that happened at work on a particular day. These issues may have been small or incidental, but the problem, in my mind, was a mountain. Let us emphasize that: <u>IN MY MIND</u>.

I think a lot of things that happened in my mind in the past were due to a lack of confidence in **myself**. When a person would say something that might have not meant anything, I created a story about it and made a mountain. I believe that we make our own mountains and obstacles in our minds.

In my case, were these things really mountains? Nope. Do you have mountains you face each day? After all these years, I have learned that we should reevaluate our mountains. I do not believe we ever face an unsolvable problem. For example, John F. Kennedy gave a speech in 1962 at Rice University where he said the United States needed to land a man on the moon. He would not accept those who said it could not be done. People worked and they achieved the "impossible". They sent that man to the moon. They, like many others in history, have accomplished feats that may have seemed impossible for a time.

Again, I truly believe that there are no problems that are unsolvable. If we put our mind to it, I know we can personally conquer anything we believe to be a difficulty or an obstacle. We just have to take a step back, evaluate the situation, identify options, and then move forward. Staying in the same place is not an option. Ignoring situations do not work. Any situation, whatever it is, does not change until you make it change.

Believe it or not, in my experience, it is generally simple to initiate change. I believe it is better to start with <u>something</u> versus doing <u>nothing</u>, no matter how small the start for improvement may be. Two key words: <u>identify</u> and <u>start</u>. Nothing happens without some type of action and commitment, whether personally or in a business situation.

And so it evolved. . . It took me many years to start to use my quality improvement process thinking to identify that MY behaviors and feelings had a root cause. I was in a rut and I did not even know it. I lost myself in my day to day routine, just going through the actions. Do you feel this way? I was getting up in the morning, going to work, coming home, caring for the kids, and falling into bed exhausted only to get up and do it again the next day. The days turned into weeks, months, years. I was always working: during vacations, during car trips, during weekends. Every time I turned around it was Friday, and it ALWAYS seemed to be Christmas again! Sound familiar yet? I now ask myself how I allowed this to happen. I know now that I was too busy. I was engrossed in <u>PROVING</u> I was a worthy person to everyone else but myself, the one who really mattered. Further, I did not rely on anyone else. I was proud that I was able to do it all, which I now realize also created social isolation. I had no time to spare for anything except taking care of all the "stuff" I had to do.

Here is the quick story of how I woke up. Once in a while my husband and I had our parents babysit the kids so we could take a weekend away alone here and there. This time, our kids were a little older, with our oldest son starting college. We decided to leave them alone for a few days to go on a trip, just the two of us. We have been motorcycle enthusiasts since we were teens and we packed up our Goldwing and went to a motorcycle rally in Lake George. That year, I believe, there were approximately 38,000 attendees. I never saw so many motorcycles in one place. It was an amazing event, just people who loved to ride, not the stereotypical image of motorcyclists – no rowdiness, no trouble. After all, most motorcyclists are professional, everyday people enjoying a hobby (like us!).

Here we were, riding along with the others. Then it hit me. These people were taking "time to play" and enjoying a passion! It hit me more after we parked and took off our helmets, and I started to look around at the others who parked and took off their helmets. I realized that we were part of the minority of the attendees. I believed Jim and I were among the youngest there.

I understand that there are obligations for people and they cannot necessarily just up and leave their kids to go on a motorcycle rally. After all, we had wanted to go to this rally for years but did not because we had to care for our kids and other obligations. The primary point I am making here is <u>WHEN</u> do we take "time to play"? When do we start to enjoy life before it is too late?

My wheels started turning. With the way I worked, and the way I thought and strived with little downtime, I realized I was headed to be one of "those people" who try to fit everything in at the end of my life instead of just taking time to enjoy everything <u>DURING</u> my life.

Since then I have taken on a new hobby, my "quest for quality of life". I started going to seminars and workshops for self improvement, and I have been reading books by people including Joel Osteen, Dr. Wayne W. Dyer, Eckert Tolle, Dr. Norman Vincent Peale, and more. My objective shifted from just going through the motions to learning how to enjoy life.

Each and every one of us started as a blank slate. With our life circumstances, we experienced things and learned things. <u>IN OUR OWN EYES</u> we may believe we have failed. It is our beliefs about ourselves, the world and other circumstances that motivate us to action. I value the lessons of others and have been learning from those who went through similar growth processes. And, with a quality improvement process in mind, once someone has identified a deficiency and implement changes, we can learn from them to cut out some time, right?

Unfortunately as I speak with people, many are going through the same or similar circumstances, but learning how to improve things may not necessarily be recognized as a priority. There are volumes of writings about how people would rather complain than change. We know them. . . whiners, cry babies, "drama kings/queens". . . or maybe we are one of them. I know I was. My problems were HUGE, remember? Mountains! Maybe it was done to seek attention, or maybe I did not know how to initiate change. Are we taught to be dependent and powerless vs. independent and strong? When we dwell on our problems or complain about things we become increasingly powerless.

Who is teaching these empowering skills to us so we can initiate change and have a better life? I realized it would be wonderful to have a bank of experts where people can learn what they need to know so they can enjoy life and then be able to have quality of life. I came up with the Time to Play Philosophy realizing people cannot "play" if they are not healthy, happy, have money or a work life balance. I have been putting this bank of experts together so we can have a hub of resources to achieve a better quality of life.

No matter the number of resources out there, no matter what anyone tells you, no matter what health issues you face, no matter how many people try to hold you back, the first step will always be to identify that you are ready to change in the first place. We need to realize we are partaking in a behavior that is limiting our ability to enjoy life so we can change. . . before it is too late. Thankfully, in my situation, my eyes were opened. Having regrets is not on my radar.

I should note, as it relates to the Time to Play Philosophy that people will tell me, "I do not need money to be happy". I hear it all the time. I beg to differ. You <u>DO</u> need money. Can you have quality of life if you do not know where the next dollar will come from so you can feed your kids or pay your mortgage or rent? Or would that make you sick and stressed? It is up to you to determine the answer. Like it or not, money takes care of our needs.

Resolving that we all need money to survive in our society, perhaps the biggest obstacle many of us face is the confidence to realize we are worthy to be paid for what we provide. I have always been scared to ask for salary because I did not have enough **confidence** that I **could** ask. Not only could I not ask, which made me feel badly and taken advantage of, but I would justify things so it was not my fault. I would also justify requesting a lower salary or fee, for example, "They are a not for profit, and they do not have money to pay, so I will charge less." Every organization has money to pay if they really want a product or service and will always find a way to get it done.

BUT — not if you do not ask for it! Why would they pay more than you ask? And, of course we pride ourselves on the game of negotiation, of who can get something for less money. Look at the car commercials negotiating for the best deal. We do it with everything, including people, and brag about it saying things like, "I am only paying $___, isn't that great"? In my opinion, we have devalued a lot in our society by always looking for the cheaper price. It is actually a recognized philosophy known as the Wal-Mart mentality.

I have realized we need to <u>ASK</u> for what we need, want, and are worth. The bottom line: If we do not ask, I believe it truly hurts us deep inside and strips us of our self worth and our self esteem. Just a quick disclaimer: Do not just go barging into your boss's office on Monday demanding a huge raise and say that Doreen said so. You have to do some research first. We might believe we are worth a million dollars (and we probably are), but we have to also consider what the market and the organization where we work will bear. Nevertheless, remember that you always have a choice. You can look for another job, or you can open your own business. If you are not happy, do not stay stuck. Identify what is the cause of your unhappiness and start to determine the things you can do to change your circumstances. Then initiate a change to make your life better so you can enjoy life.

Asking for what you need does not have to be just money related. It can be in any aspect of your life. What have you not asked for? Do you feel terrible inside when you do not ask for what you want? I know I do. Look deep. Look for the root cause of what is making you unhappy. Again, you need to identify what the source is in order to get rid of it and move on to a more fulfilling life.

As you know, I had become obsessed striving for the "brass ring", looking for ways to satisfy myself. When one thing was finished, I would move on to the next, because the feelings that I was "good" or the "high" I felt when I accomplished something did not last. I became a junkie, of sorts. I had to hear someone tell me I did a good job, or get a pat on the back, or achieve some type of recognition to prove it to myself, ALL OF THE TIME. "It would be great when

_____ happens," I would think. I would validate things like, "If only I got this position," "If only we got that house," "If only I could _____." You can fill in the blanks to suit your needs as I did for many years.

Achievement became my vice. Do you have a vice? Some of us eat to feel better and cover up pain. Some gamble for the rush, shop, do drugs, or drink to "fit in" or to forget. We use material things to feel good about ourselves or to cover up something we do not want to address. This temporarily takes away our pain, but it does not really help in the long run. The feeling of not being confident or not being good enough down deep does not go away. We look for ways to fit in somewhere, to be a part of something, but, in our minds, we remain an outsider and just do not fit in.

If this sounds like you, as it was me, maybe it is time to ask how we think our life is going so far. Take a look around. Sometimes we know our behavior or feelings are undesirable. I think those of us who recognize this happen to be the lucky ones. We have made the first step to change. What do we do about it? Hopefully we start to make things change for the better so we can enjoy life.

Sometimes we do nothing because we do not know how to take the first step and start to change. Sometimes we continue the vicious cycle of our life situation. We continue the same way we learned, and our kids continue what they learn and what they see from us, and history repeats itself. History should not repeat. History should be a platform for growth and change. We know what works and what does not.

The Pilgrim Philosophy

Any time I tell someone about my "pilgrim philosophy" analogy, I always preempt my discussion with a disclaimer, "Without you thinking I have gone off the deep end." It just hit me one day, and I felt it was an important thought to add into this chapter.

So, with my disclaimer, and without you thinking I have gone off the deep end, I came up with this thought process. When the pilgrims came to America and we settled in this Country, I believe we depended on each other for survival. We had jobs to accomplish and places to live. We <u>all were needed and had a function and **we depended on each other**</u>, hence, the "pilgrim philosophy".

What has happened to us? In my opinion, and through my observations, I believe we have gotten away from this principal. Instead, many of us have become dependent or isolated and alone. We strive on our own. Many of us have lost our sense of community. We are stressed out. I might go so far as to talk about how people have become disempowered. With almost 47 million people[4] in our society in the year 2011 being under poverty level, there has to be a level of disempowerment. In the recent political races, you hear how many jobs the President or elected officials are going to make. Why should they make jobs for us? Is it possible for us to create our own jobs? The pilgrims did not have anyone making jobs for them, did they? And, to boot, governmental programs that pay people have to be funded by, guess who, us. So, we have to work harder to pay for other people to have jobs. This is just a personal realization that I had that I wanted to share, and you may agree or disagree.

For those people who may be living in an undesirable situation, they may also feel alone or not know where to turn. They may feel trapped. That is my point. We can always seek help or change – IF we want to. But, that is the key right there. We have to WANT to. You have heard that one before. We need to remember that we live in America; a place I believe remains a land of opportunity. I truly hope that there is always a way out or a way to change our circumstances, but it must begin with our decision to do so. **"You can lead a horse to water but you cannot make him drink".**

And, let us discuss the incredibly competitive atmosphere out there. Our kids are taught to compete from the moment they come out of the womb. I remember our pediatrician asking me how my first child was doing when I brought him in for checkups. I felt compelled to brag about his accomplishments even though she was just inquiring about markers to check on his development. After all, my kid was the best, right? What causes this behavior?

What happens when we play a game. . . any game? We want to win. You know who you are! Even if you are playing with your kids, something in you wants to win. Do not even come near us when my husband and I are playing a game! Or, there were the times I would be the one telling my kids to "play nice", but there I would be, "rooting" them on (perhaps an understatement) during a soccer game, a competition, or whatever the circumstance.

Winner takes all, right? This is what we learn and what we see. I am not saying we should not strive to be the best we can be, but winning seems to be epidemic in our society. Competition may be pushing us past what we can reasonably achieve as human beings to a point where we cannot reach. Look at Lance Armstrong and the other sports heroes that have gone to extremes using drugs to achieve feats greater than humanly possible. Look at the recent finance moguls that significantly and adversely affected millions of people through their greed and quest for profits. Look at our political elections which are getting more vicious with each race. Are we teaching our kids that we should go to any lengths to win, no matter what?

It is a very foreign concept for people when I say "collaboration = success" to people, and I am usually met with a "what is in it for me" attitude or comment. This blows my mind. I love the T-E-A-M concept, but in my experience at work, it has been more of a blame game. Everyone wants to look better than the next person, almost to the point of sabotage. As long as you look good, right? It does not matter, right?

I sometimes wonder if people remember how it was when they first started out. How they felt when they opened their business. How they felt when they got their first job or first job interview. In today's society, the competition begins younger and younger. We put so much stress on ourselves and our kids with "healthy competition". Is it so healthy? Or, does it rob us of enjoyment and cause stress.

Perhaps it would be wonderful, instead, if people would take you under their wing and mentor you and help you out. Remember apprenticeships from the old days? Although some stories we may have learned about in history class where apprenticeships were not all ideal, the concept of being an apprentice to learn a skill to succeed in life is a great concept. I wish I had sought this type of experience when I was younger. I know there are internship and job shadowing opportunities available. However, I wonder how much of a priority it is to implement these types of programs or how visible the opportunities are to our students or those starting a new career.

And, then there's the networking. I have stopped going to many events, as over the years, people I have met would rather sell to you than talk with you. I actually have had people walk up to me and say, "I'm a competitor of yours." I believe it would be much nicer if people would give each other advice about how they succeeded or, perhaps, make introductions to someone who could take you or your business to the next level. I am not saying this does not happen. It does. But I have seen so many people struggle. I have noted previously that I believe everyone has something to offer that can help another. In my case, my word is gold. I will never tell someone I will do something and not follow-through. Have you seen someone you could have helped but just let the opportunity pass by? Are you too worried about yourself or your own "stuff" to really take notice of or follow-through to help another?

Again, my platform is "collaboration = success". If we listened and learned what someone else does, we might be able to work together and grow our own companies or help someone cut some time off their efforts to help them succeed. I have always had this thought since starting our business: that we could work with other companies and grow, that we could combine the efforts between companies through strategic alliances and work together to make our businesses bigger and bring in bigger clients. Unfortunately, in my experience I have found people who have their "hands out" looking for salary instead of wanting to build something together. Nevertheless, I keep the idea of "collaboration = success" foremost in my vision. I know it is the right way and will always look for opportunities to work together with others to become stronger. Remember the common statement:

Many hands make light work ~ Unknown

Somewhere in our past this was identified. Someone said it. This is another example of the teachings of our elders. Why has this been forgotten? I can give more personal examples of the loss of "many hands make light work", but I do not think I need to. Just think about your own experiences in your current or past job, or your participation in an organization or a club, and I'm sure you can identify some yourself. I have personally heard, "It is not my job," or had people who rather crush you than work together so they could shine. Without generalizing, it seems there is always a core group of people or a committee who do all the work, usually comprised of the same individuals time and again. We all have been part of groups where we have experienced people who believe others "owe" it to them to get things done and then they just show up. Sometimes people are even angry if it is not done right, but ask them to take over and see what type of response you will get. Just ask my mother and father-in-law who are coordinators of a large senior group. They have a hard time getting people to pitch in to do the legwork, but people always are there to reap the benefits.

What happened to working together for the whole? For the good of an organization? For the good of a community? *Where are our pilgrims? Where is our TEAM?*

While we have touched on the topic of people who would rather crush you so they can shine, I would like to bring up discussion on the expression: **Words Cut Like a Knife**

Again, each time I write one of these common expressions, I wish I knew where some of these phrases originated, who said them for the first time and what the circumstance surrounding the statement had been. We are going to come back to "words cut like a knife" in the final chapter of this book, but I needed to also bring it up here. Remember my "tortured soul" observation? We have to identify when we are being tortured to change what we are allowing inside our head. Both of these concepts, the words cut like a knife and being a tortured soul have a connection.

I recently met a woman in her eighties. We were talking about New Year's resolutions and this lovely woman told me her New Year's resolution, which was to. . . *let things go in one ear and out the other.*

I'm not kidding. Even in her later years, she is still dealing with people telling her things that make her upset and feel bad. I recently realized how important it is to notice what people say and how it affects us. Don't let their words cut you like a knife. I also realized the importance of noticing our feelings after being with someone. My New Year's resolution this year was to eliminate the people in my life who make me feel bad about myself. We each know who these people are in our lives. We get that twinge inside after we visit or talk with them. They might zap our energy, or we might feel horrible in some other way after communicating with them. This was a change I decided to make for me.

In the event they cannot completely be eliminated, it might be necessary to take steps to prepare to remain empowered before going to visit or meet with them, relatives too! Here is an example. I was talking to another woman in her eighties that began telling me how she feels when she visits with her sister, the "smart one". I asked her why her sister was the "smart one". She said because her sister always says so. Keep in mind that we cannot change our relatives, and, for prosperity, we might not be able to completely cut them out of our lives. I suggested that she needed to identify positive things about herself that she knows about herself to prepare for their visits to keep her empowered, for example: that she is strong, smart, beautiful, etc. You get the idea. In this case, she knows that she is smart. She IS smart. However, she does not feel smart when she is around her sister – she feels intimidated and bad about herself. Why do we allow others to steal our power and our voice? Why do we allow others to make us feel bad? **Key word: ALLOW**.

No one can actually steal our power or our voice or make us feel bad on their own; we ALLOW them to take it away. I told her to take an index card and to write her true empowering beliefs and strengths on it. In her case, things like I am smart, strong, powerful, beautiful, etc. I suggested she read the index card before she sees her sister and then to read it after their visit. If it is necessary, it can easily be read *during* their visit if the disempowering starts with a quick trip to the rest room! **DO NOT let anyone steal your power.** You always have to remember **you are AMAZING**. There is no one else in this world like you.

Be amazing!

Through my quest for quality of life, a recurrent theme I have been hearing is about people's lack of self worth or their lack of confidence. When we do not have self worth or self confidence we may tend to create stories about what we think others think about us. I can truly admit that I was lacking in both of these areas, and sometimes still allow my thoughts to get the best of me. However, I have become aware when this happens and can generally stop the stories before they begin blossoming. Have you ever thought: What if they do not like me? What if I am not good enough? What will they think? What will they say? What if I do not fit in?

So, have you thought these things? If they say it, after all, it must be so, right? Who are "they" anyway? And, why do we care? Why do we worry? Why do we stress? Why does it matter so much?

I do have to say that I am very proud of my eighteen year old daughter, Jacquelyn. She does not care or listen to what "they" say. She is her own person with her own sense of style, and she pursues things that make her happy. She does not allow what others say to change or sway what she does. One thing she has identified is that she does not like "hanging out" with a lot of the kids that she knows. In her observations, they have so many issues they are just not fun to be around. Jacquelyn has confidence in herself and she has self-love. We have always supported our kids in their passions and their endeavors, so I get where the self-love came from. She must have learned the self-confidence from her father. I am not putting myself down. I am a work in progress and am proud to be in the place I am in now. I recognize that I have come so far. But, observing Jacquelyn and her actions has made me think and realize that self confidence and self-love are key, and something we all need to have in our lives.

Chapter 10

I Believe Everything Happens for a Reason

❦

Contributor: Christine Farrell-Guma

I have known Chrissy since I was 18 years old. She married my husband's brother Tommy a year before Jim and I were married. We have always had a connection even though we have spent many years separated by the distance between New York and North Carolina.

Although we do not talk as often as I would like, I knew about her struggles with her job. She works hard, like so many others, but still remains unfulfilled. I recognize how hard it was for her to go through her own physical disappointments and her father's illness and death. She knows I am always here for her, a cheerleader in her corner.

When I first started Time to Play, Chrissy was one of the first people I reached out to. I asked her to start the positive quote or thought of the day. She does this splendidly. Every day, no matter what, Chrissy provides inspiration to others. She constantly reminds people that they are strong and valuable and that they can enjoy their life. Through helping each other we help ourselves, and the positive thoughts of the day have sparked strength in Chrissy, as well. She has made noticeable improvements in her quality of life in the recent past. She has been able to let go of things that held her back. As we previously discussed, our thoughts, which are most powerful, can provoke such distress in us that they may cause us to live as a victim and can hold us back from enjoying life.

As you read Chrissy's chapter you will learn about an experience she had in her teens that "haunted" her for years keeping her a prisoner in her mind. What holds you back? What haunts you? Is it time to break free? We all deserve to enjoy life. The key is to learn what it is that holds us back. I am so thankful that she has broken the chains that held her, and that she can now move forward.

I thank Chrissy for her story and hope her experience can create hope for you or a loved one. Hope, even after holding on to something for many years, that it is never too late to change your thinking and to release your self-created captivity.

— Doreen

When Doreen asked me if I wanted to write a chapter for her book I immediately said yes. How could I not be part of her story or project that, in the end, has ultimately helped me?

I had a great childhood. I am so thankful that I can look back at my childhood and remember all of the great vacations, summers, etc. My Mom was always home, dinner was always on the table at six o'clock p.m., and the house was always clean. I always saw my parents holding hands, showing affection and knew someday that was what I wanted. I idolized my father. He was everything that I was not. He was strong, fearless, and a mover. He always had to have something to do, but did enjoy watching his sports games over the weekend. I can remember waiting up when he was on the night shift to make sure he came home okay. As soon as he pulled into the driveway I would be sound asleep. To me, it was a storybook childhood. I thought that since my childhood was so great, so would be my future. I learned that would not become my reality.

I graduated from high school in 1984. I had a great job after high school and a wonderful boyfriend who would soon become my husband. This is when things started to become troubling to me. I worked for a company on Long Island for about six months. One of the guys in the warehouse would come and sit with the staff at break time. He always seemed to sit next to me, but I did not think anything of it at the time. This all happened the year that Hurricane Gloria hit Long Island. I headed into work that morning since they said that the storm was not going to hit until late that afternoon. Somehow this guy in the warehouse was able to get my home phone number from the human resources department. He stated that he would call to tell me not to come in. Why they gave it to him is one of those things I will never know, but it began a nightmare for me. After I left that job, I got a job working for a brokerage firm, which I loved. This guy must have followed me home one day, because when my husband dropped me off after a date one night he was sitting in his car right down the street. My husband (then boyfriend) got behind him and followed him to the expressway. This man would continue to show up at my workplace up until the day we moved to North Carolina. He would show up and every day one of the male employees would walk me to my car and make sure I got started off okay. I am sure this guy is long gone and he does not even know who I am anymore, but he never left my mind. I have never really spoken about this, but it has been something that left me feeling powerless in life.

My husband and I were married in April of 1987. Soon after, my parents retired to North Carolina. They loved it there, and we decided to move to be with them. The move let me put the past behind me and to move forward to something fresh and new. We both found good jobs and made new friends, and although we missed our family and friends back in New York immensely, we knew this was a great move for us. We were eager to start a family. I had always joked with Tommy that I wanted us to have a minibus full of kids.

He did not quite want so many, but children were what we both wanted. One year turned into two years which turned into three years. I thought, "Okay, time for us to both get checked out." All the tests came back normal, so we tried again. After a couple of heartbreaking miscarriages I was finally pregnant. We could not be any happier, and when my son Andrew was born, it was truly the most wonderful thing that had ever happened in my life. It was now the three of us! We started to plan on when to have the next baby, which we wanted pretty quickly. Unfortunately, it was not meant to be. I had to have a partial hysterectomy at the age of thirty-five. It took a long time for me to accept the fact that I would not have another child, but my son is great, and with him I felt fulfilled.

Around 1994 my Father became ill. It started with slurred speech, then loss of mobility. I watched a man who was fifty when he became ill become a shell of himself by the time he was fifty-seven. He was diagnosed with Severe Parkinsonism, and it chipped away at his whole body. The worst part of it all was not being able to hear my father's voice ever again. At that point in my life I was raising a toddler, working a full-time job as an Operations Manager, trying to be a good wife, and trying to be a good daughter. Whenever there was a medical emergency I was there. My mom would sometimes forget to ask questions since she was caught up in the moment. I became my father's voice. I learned to stand up to the doctors and nurses when they did not want one extra person in his room. I went as high as the hospital president to get approval to be in his room at all times. The one thing I found odd at that time is that my son was a little over two and had not really been talking. He had numerous ear infections when he was a baby, and the doctor thought that he was behind in his progress. We noticed that Andrew had started talking around the time my father stopped, which left a lasting impression on me.

We were with my father when he passed away in June of 2000 after a seven year battle. It was very peaceful, and he was surrounded by love. Life started to go back to our "new normal", and then I got laid off from my job where I had been a loyal employee for twenty years.

I was so strong through everything else in my life, but this put me into a downward spiral that I could not climb out of. I tried, but did not want to talk to anyone or see anyone. It was like everything that had bothered me, the infertility, my dad getting sick, the anger of being stalked, the frustration of giving my life to a job for twenty years only to be let go, all came rushing out.

It has taken me a long time to realize that some of these events made me even stronger, and Doreen's project has been a huge help with this. I stopped giving my stalker room to still make me feel powerless. He was not worthy of any of my emotions at this point it my life. He was gone. Suffering through infertility was very depressing. I could harp on that the rest of my life, but I realized that I am so blessed to have a smart, kind, and compassionate child that I am so very proud of. Why should I be sad? I should not be, and I am no longer affected! Through my father's sickness I found my own voice. I found that I can do anything I need to in order to help the people that I love. I did not really care what anyone thought of me. I just wanted them to help my father. I learned to speak up for myself, which was something I was never able to do previously.

I have reinvented my life, and I am now working for myself to help people with their needs. I did not want to go back to work for someone to use my talent and then let me go. It is time for me to use my talents for my family, and I look forward to the next half of my life.

I know sometimes we get busy and that there is not always a lot of time to enjoy life. I make time for myself now, even if it is only ten minutes a day. At this time my son is approaching his twenty-first birthday. My baby grew up so fast, and as a result of my internal battles, I just sit back and wonder how much I missed. I am done missing anything any longer.

To the reader of this book, I hope you can believe that you can turn your life around. I am going to be forty-seven this year. I know it is not too late.

Take time out to play every day, even for ten minutes. Do something that gives you peace: read a book, take a bath, do something just for <u>YOU</u>! I am proof that we can get through a lot of terrible things that happen in life. I believe that if God brings you to it, He will bring you through it. He never gives you more than you can handle. Always try to remember that. I also could not have gone through any of this without the love and support of my husband who has gone above and beyond the call of husband and son-in-law. I have learned that I am truly blessed in my life, and for that I am thankful.

I hope you can realize that you are blessed, as well. If we look for it, we can all find something to be thankful for. This is my wish for you.

Chapter 11

Lost. . . Then Found

ౖ⁂ఌ

Contributor: Jonathan S. Barrett

I would like you to meet Jonathan Barrett, my brother. I asked him to write a chapter for *If I Knew Then What I Know Now* to share his experience with depression, thoughts of suicide, and how he grew and unearthed his faith in God through his experience.

A few months ago, after a discussion I had with my daughter and some research I did, I started asking people if they knew the statistics of suicide and depression in our society. I asked elected officials, school administrators and regular people. From the feedback I received, the people who actually know about the prevalence of suicide and depression in our society are far and few between.

Why? I believe it is a topic that remains taboo. Sure, there are commercials about the wonderful medications you can take to help you with your depression, but how many people know the numbers of those affected? We hear about the number of people who get breast cancer, the number of people with heart disease, but we do not *really* hear about depression and suicide.

Because it is not a subject we talk about, I believe people with suicidal thoughts and depression become isolated. People may feel embarrassed and keep their feelings hidden. Does the taboo nature of the illness keep people from seeking help until it is, perhaps, too late? How did this become so taboo? Perhaps it is the stigma created by movies where people with psychiatric illness are locked away, or perhaps it is the horrible stories about the psychiatric hospitals that we have all heard about.

We have to stop being embarrassed and fearful and start to discuss suicide and depression in our society. We are all here to help each other, right? The statistics of the prevalence in our society demand that this must become a forefront of conversation. Perhaps, if it was not hidden, we would have people who were not isolated or alone with their feelings of hopelessness or helplessness and we could circumvent some negative outcomes or suffering from those with depression or thoughts of suicide.

As I noted, I knew nothing about the statistics or the prevalence of the numbers of people affected in our society until June, 2012. During a discussion I had with my daughter, she told me about so many children in her school she knew who already had a "what's the use" attitude towards life. She knew kids who had, at such a young age, no desire to strive to get ahead. I was quite saddened by our discussion and started to ask questions. My son in college told me the same thing that he had noticed about some of his peers. Many of his friends, he told me, know that it is hard to find jobs, and many view the job opportunities as low paying or without job security. He said that many have given up before they have even gotten started. And, he was not the only one, either. Once I started asking, these same sentiments were conveyed by other teens and young adults. We put so much pressure on ourselves. I believe we were put on this planet to enjoy life, not to be tortured souls, but some of us have allowed ourselves to become disempowered. We have allowed our minds to tell us stories causing so many among us to become sick and sad.

From the published articles I have read, suicide is 100% preventable; however, the statistics regarding the number of people who consider or commit suicide in today's society are alarming. The Center for Disease Control (CDC) published that, in 2007, suicide was the third leading cause of death for young people ages 15 to 24, the second leading cause of death in colleges, and that for every suicide completion, there are between 50 and 200 attempts. The CDC performed a youth risk survey which showed that 8.5% of students in grades 9-12 reported a suicide attempt in the past year and that 25% of high school students report suicide ideation (thoughts). Probably the most disturbing was their notation that a recent survey of high school students found that almost

1 in 5 had seriously considered suicide, more than 1 in 6 had made plans to attempt suicide, and more than 1 in 12 had made a suicide attempt in the past year.

Additionally, the CDC noted that, of every 100,000 people ages 65 and older, 14.3 died by suicide in 2007 and that, in the general population, there were 11.3 suicides per 100,000 people. In 2007 suicide was the 10th leading death in our population overall.[5] Again, we hear about the prevalence of so many disease processes and cancers. We DO NOT hear about the silent killer that is suicide. We need to hear about this.

In regards to depression, in July of 2011, the CDC posted statistics that depression affects 1 in 10 United States adults[6], and the National Institute of Mental Health (NIMH) posted that approximately 11.2% of 13 to 18 year olds in the United States are affected by depressive disorders[7]. There is a lot of research on these statistics available, and I invite you to look further into the topic if you so desire. I believe it is very important that we know more so we can help others.

Jonathan's Chapter, *Lost. . . Then Found* discusses his journey, what he learned, and how he found his faith in Jesus. His story is extremely powerful.

I am truly embarrassed, but have to note that, when I heard he was brought to the psychiatric unit, I became "para-lyzed" and remember ignoring the situation. Even after so many years working in health care, I did not know what to do, how to handle it, or what to say. I am hoping that can change as we start to discuss this. What are we supposed to do? How do you approach someone who wanted to commit suicide? Do you ask questions and talk about it?

Perhaps, through this chapter, we can begin to learn, as a community of people, what to do and how to extend support, an embrace, or fill a need for someone hurting so badly.

I am so very proud of Jonathan and his strength. I am thankful and grateful for his wife, Sarah, who has stood by him. We all need people to support us in our lives so we are not alone, and Jonathan is blessed by not only having support in the physical realm, but the spiritual realm. I am proud to present *Lost. . . Then Found*.

— Dawer

Just Barely Hanging On: It seemed like a New York minute. Before I could even gasp for air I had finished my undergraduate degree at the University of Alabama and was working for a mammoth advertising agency in the Mecca they call Manhattan. I had made it. Status and pride filled my existence at the fact that I was an advertising buff on the biggest stage at age twenty-two. Little did I know the show would last fifteen hours daily and that I would become basically non-existent to my wife, Sarah and our one month old baby girl at home. The aura of business superstardom began to wear off after a few months as I saw my life developing into the likes of a gigantic Rocky Mountain avalanche. As I looked around the train during my daily four hour roundtrip journey back and forth to and from Penn Station I began to feel like Bill Murray in the movie *Groundhog Day*. What I saw every day was misery. I saw exhaustion on human faces. Even more frightening, I saw my future. I overheard many conversations on the train occupied by the same people daily. Most of the stories sung the same tune: Divorced a time or two, veterans of this same commute for thirty-five years, searching for purpose and lasting joy, and duped into thinking "once upon a time" that money and status could buy fulfillment.

Before long I turned into an insomniac, shaking with anxiety in my bed as my blood shot eyes were polarized by my alarm clock turning from 5:29 to 5:30 a.m. Was it time to go already? I just got home six hours ago! My life was about getting up at 5:30 a.m., a four hour roundtrip commute to the Mecca, coming home after 11 o'clock p.m., seeing Sarah for less than one hour, and kissing my already sleeping daughter for the first time in the day. If you are wondering what tomorrow was like, just rinse and repeat. Questions began to enter my mind that I honestly never thought about before because I was the captain of my ship. I was on a course to gain status in this life. What *really* was the meaning of life? *Why* was I here? *Was this all there is*?As I kept going back and forth to the city daily, these questions began to ring louder in my mind. What happened next turned my world upside down. I came in as a "big shot" but I began to lose favor at work due to my inexperience and pride. I found my career at one of the biggest and best advertising agencies crumbling before my eyes. I was losing my identity. During my daily commute I had more than enough time to think. Believe me. The pressure mounted and I was like a man trying to lift a boulder with two broken arms. Not long after, things turned for the worse. I faced the reality of losing my job, and this once shiny wheel was now rusty and squeaky. My status dissipated. Depression, panic, anxiety, and thoughts of suicide rushed in. My life would be better off over and done with rather than losing my identity as an aspiring giant in the business world.

The breaking point came, and like a gust of wind during a category five hurricane, I found myself at the hospital in the psych ward. I was in disbelief. Here I was: depressed, suicidal, and unable to go on any longer. I was a long way from the successful bright lights of big business Manhattan and what I thought the canvas of my life was destined to look like. My life seemed to go from being a Picasso to a wet painting, and here I was, watching with tears as the colors smeared off the canvas of my life. As I headed home with my new reality I found myself unable to get out of bed. Sarah painfully looked on at what was now barely a shell of the man she married. I caused the woman I loved severe anguish. The shell of me was hollow. There was nothing left.

As I was lifeless in my bed with plenty of time to think, those old questions started ringing in my head again: What *really* was the meaning of life? *Why* was I here? I literally felt a gaping hole in my heart and soul. I cried out in anguish as pieces of myself, and the man I was, became unglued. The hole was a shape that I was not familiar with. Nothing I tried to stuff into it would fit. I felt like a lost puzzle where all of the pieces had jagged edges that would not fit together. Sarah looked on with tears in her eyes as I continued this trend for a week. I could not eat, I could not sleep, and my mind would not turn from the marathon movie of severe depression. In my mind I could hear screaming and shrieking: "S-u-i-c-i-d-e." The toll was being taken on my marriage and my family. What happened next was more unlikely than anything I could have ever imagined. In fact, on a scale of one to ten of "very unlikely" to "very likely" it was no more than a zero.

I grew up without a spiritual background, so when thoughts of God entered into my mind I became alarmed and scared. I began to talk to Sarah about these thoughts and she began to pray for me secretly. Sarah had a short period of straying from God, like many do, who want to find fulfillment in the world away from God. It did not take long for her to see that the world without God was empty. She came back to fellowship with God stronger than ever, and kept praying for me and loving me selflessly, even though I had nothing to give. As I said, I had no spiritual background and no knowledge of God. I did not even know who Jesus Christ was and had never even picked up a Bible or any other "religious" book, for that matter. Lovingly Sarah told me bits and pieces about God and how this hole I had in my life was something only He could fill because I was created by Him. I still remained skeptical, and although I was listening to her, the words simply fell on deaf ears.

New Life

As the depression raged on and suicide continued to scream my name, an indescribable moment occurred. I could not be more truthful when I say that it was almost as if I felt a hand or a loud voice that said, "Get up!" I obeyed, getting out of bed and falling to my knees in tears in front of Sarah. I told her I could not do *this* without God anymore, and whoever He was, I needed Him in my life. I remember crying out, "I cannot do this anymore without God," several times. This road led right to Jesus Christ and I immediately asked Sarah for a Bible. I never read a real book in my entire life. Through kindergarten to twelfth grade, and even through college, I got by on something called "Cliffs Notes". But now, here I was, unbelievably crying out for a Bible. I could hardly believe the words that were coming out my mouth. Sarah gave me her Bible and told me to borrow it for as long as I wanted. I clenched it against my chest and refused to let it go.

She had a trip scheduled to go home to Alabama long before any of this happened and refused to leave me in my current state. I had to basically force her to go. I remember confidently convincing her that I was fine now and that she should not miss spending time with her family. I told her I was going to find a church while she was gone, which really caught her off guard. That is exactly what I did. I read her Bible day and night studying God's every Word. I started out reading the Book of John and quickly discovered the definition of an ugly world that nailed Jesus to the cross called "sin". Immediately I knew I was guilty of sin as even the "whitest" of lies, smallest rage of anger, or one tiny adulterous thought kept me from measuring up from the standard of a perfect God. Also, there was no amount of good deeds that I could "do" to "earn" my way into heaven or to have a relationship with God. I was very distraught by this because I was desperate to prove something. Then I read a verse that is often seen on signs at football games: John 3:16, "For God so loved the world that He gave His only Son (Jesus) that whoever believes in Him shall not perish but have everlasting life". To get this baffling concept straight in my mind, I read it out loud again. I was baffled at the fact that God loved me so much that He allowed Jesus to die on the cross to pay for my sins so that I, Jonathan Barrett, would spend eternity now and forever with Him. How could this be? I wanted in on this deal immediately.

This moment was the start of my life. Yes, I was born physically on June, 27 1979 but now I was born for real. The hole in my heart was finally not empty anymore. I would like to say that at this point everything turned out smelling like roses and we all lived happily ever after, but the only way to bend iron is to heat it up. My depression was still alive and kicking and it was something God would use to bend and shape me. I had no idea what church to go to and decided to attend a small Baptist church on Long Island, New York only because it was located on the same street where my sister lived.

I made my mother attend church with me because I was embarrassed to go alone and Sarah was still out of town visiting family. My mother reluctantly came with me, and four men immediately approached us as we entered the door. With smiling faces, it was like they had known me my whole life. Two Franks, a Bob, and a Rich introduced themselves to me. Little did they know they were taking on a broken mess who had just come to faith in Jesus Christ. Before the church service started I was freaking out. I had never attended a church service before so I was shy and skeptical. But there was something so real about these men that calmed my fears. I wanted what they had. They invited me to a men's Bible study as we spoke and I told my story. This was exactly what I needed. I found it odd that I was not ashamed to tell my story. I felt some things were embarrassing like how I was currently as depressed as anyone could be and freshly out of the hospital after dealing with struggles of wanting to end it all. But I could not stop telling others about the new hope that Jesus had given me.

The Transformation: When Sarah came back home from visiting her family I told her about the church and we started attending every Sunday. I attended the Bible study every week with the two Frank's, Bob, and Rich. I was broken. I needed to learn how to be a husband, a father, and wanted to learn to live life with true peace and joy. As the weeks of Bible study passed, these men mostly listened to me cry. They cried, too, because of how badly I was hurting. They prayed for me and encouraged me. I will never forget Bob's prayer for me one night going around the table. He prayed that I would see just how special God made me and that I would realize His love for me.

In the following months I started to realize small changes. For one, I previously cursed a lot but just stopped using bad language. I could not explain it. And, the more I read God's Word, the more I learned. I soaked up every bit of it like a sponge. I was getting fed for the first time in my life with lasting fulfillment, and it was not ever going away like everything else used to. The fire only started to burn brighter for my new purpose. Still, there was the issue of my depression. Why would it not go away? And why would God not just take it away? To be perfectly honest, I became frustrated and got a little angry at God. As I wrestled with Him about my depression and continued to press on and read the Bible, I happened across a passage that opened my eyes and gave me an understanding of my illness like never before.

In 2 Corinthians 12:7-10, the Apostle Paul talked about a "thorn" in his flesh. This "thorn" was something he was given to keep him from becoming conceited. Scripture does not reveal what Paul's thorn was, but most theologians believe it was perhaps chronic ophthalmia, a disease of the eyes, not extremely painful, but at times repulsive.[8] Paul pleaded with God three times to take the ailment away but God advised

Paul, "My grace is sufficient for you, for My power is made perfect in weakness". Did Paul get angry with God? No. In fact he said, "Therefore I will boast all the most gladly of my weaknesses so that the power of Christ may rest upon me. For when I am weak, then I am strong."

It was like a light went off in my head. God would use my depression and my story to help others who were going through the same thing and show them the lasting joy and peace of Jesus Christ in the life of an "ordinary Joe" like me. Did God take away my depression totally? Not entirely, but He did bring healing and victory into my life. In fact, today I can honestly say I am not depressed. God has brought me so much joy and peace because my identity is so deeply rooted in Him. Although I still struggle with depression at times, it is like night and day regarding what He has done for me and the amount of healing He has gracefully given. As part of my healing story God has taught me how to be a husband and father. Establishing a healthy household is imperative and has become a major motivating mission in my life after coming from generations of divorce in my family. The importance of a healthy marriage and its effect on my children has been one of the most rewarding experiences after ten years of marriage. A house that is firmly rooted in Christ is a house that is strong enough to weather the heavy winds of life. In a society where one out of every two marriages end in divorce, God has given Sarah and I passion to keep growing our marriage and to be an example for other couples. We have been able to pour into newly married couples and teach them how to effectively communicate and build their marriages on the unshakable foundation of Jesus Christ.

As two imperfect people coming together in marriage, it is important to actively communicate in a loving and respectful manner. A healthy marriage is living and growing, and Sarah and I found out that it takes work and commitment. Marriage is not an institution that you can put on auto-pilot and hope it works out. It takes maturity, and both parties need to be willing to work. Furthermore, God gave me this hunger which translated into studying to be a pastor with an aim at reaching and teaching families how to have a healthy home.

The Future is Now: The vision to be a pastor started in my first church on Long Island after serving as the youth group leader. Working with teenagers is perhaps one of the most rewarding things I have ever done. Teens are the most special age group of any, in my opinion. They do not realize how beautiful they are, and they are begging for love and attention. My goal was to teach my youth group just how beautiful they were to me, and more importantly, to Christ. God gave me the opportunity to teach how Jesus changes lives as I knew first hand because He was changing mine. The relationships that I made in youth group are some I will always cherish. In order to pursue the pastorate even further Sarah and I were called to Liberty University in Lynchburg, Virginia where I am currently in Seminary studying to be a pastor. Aside from serving at our local church in Lynchburg, I figured this point in my life would be a quiet one which consisted of working and going to graduate school full time. However, God truly works in amazing and unexpected ways.

A friend of mine knew of a church in Buena Vista, Virginia that had been without a pastor for four years and he and his father, who is a retired pastor, had been filling in until the church was able to get a full-time pastor. My friend was a youth pastor previously and had done most of the filling in as his father was also helping another church that was oddly in between pastors in the same area. My friend called me one day out of the blue and asked if I would be interested in helping him fill in. This was an amazing opportunity that lasted for six months. It allowed me to preach and gain invaluable experience helping others with the unchanging message of Jesus Christ amidst this world of panic and inconsistency. My time in Buena Vista came to an end in October 2012 as the church hired a full-time pastor. My time in Seminary has continued, as I now look forward to graduation. God has been preparing me to bring the message of His love to a world that is in desperate need of stability.

My "thorn" called depression occasionally rears its ugly head, but this has taught me to fully rely on God because He is in control. This illness has brought great blessing to my life. I have been able to help countless people that God has brought into my life, and it certainly keeps me humble. This falls in line with the vision God has given me for the future as a pastor where my focus will be on helping husbands and wives build successful marriages and strong legacies for their children. Additionally, due to my illness I am called to make people aware of the dangers of depression. I learned that anyone is susceptible to depression. Depression must be dealt with, not pushed under the rug as it has been in the past in our society. Helpful actions must be taken as depression is a destructive agent that tears families apart. I will continue to tell the story of my life and how God used my depression to help others and share His love. So, what is next for me and my house? We will continue to press on, anchored in Jesus Christ, and fulfill the purpose that God has made plain to us.

Chapter 12

From Hopelessness and Misery to Hope and Joy – A Story of Addiction to Laughter

Contributor: Keith Richard Godwin

*K*eith impressed me when we met. He is a tall gentleman with an amazing heart, soft spoken, kind, caring and compassionate. Before he wrote this chapter I knew some of the story about how he got to where he was, but not the full details. I thank Keith for sharing such a personal experience, what he knows now and what he went through to get there.

Keith is a veteran. I respect all veterans as they offer tremendous sacrifice for our people and our Country. Many of today's veterans are experiencing different situations after returning from combat, including lifelong physical injuries and emotional distress. Post traumatic stress disorder is recognized today as causing our veterans many hardships and suicides. Another thing that I have learned about in the recent past is of the financial hardships experienced by our veterans. A gentleman I had met a few months ago asked me if I knew how he could get help to get oil for his home, as he was concerned he and his wife would not be able to afford to heat their home. Of course I did research and found a place to refer him for help, but it made me think. Here was a man who fought for our Country and for our freedoms. How many veterans in our Country need help? It made me wonder how someone could make such a sacrifice for all of us and perhaps not have money for food or heat. I had mentioned this to an elected official and he told me that, unlike during World War II when our veterans were first and foremost in the minds of our people, today there are only 1% of families associated with military service, which is why we do not hear a lot of the issues. Going back to the concept that we are all connected and we should care about each other's plight, it does make one wonder.

However, this was not Keith's story. Keith experienced emotional trauma while growing up, which deeply affected him. His situation caused him to deal with internal struggles, and he chose alcohol and substance abuse to escape. Like many of us, we have our "self worth" battles. Keith dealt with his differently than I dealt with mine. We are all individuals and have different life situations which cause us to deal with things differently. However, you know by now that it is my hope our stories in this book will help others recognize themselves and the triggers of their self-destructive behaviors. I hope it may be their first step to healing and change.

My newly adopted motto is "learn what you need to know so you can enjoy life". We learn, we do, and we have the opportunity to change. It is always our choice.

Keith is part of Time to Play because his story and his use of laughter can help others. Sometimes our difficulties in life and the paths we follow create an amazing result. Through his struggles Keith has found a gift that he can pass along. I thank him very much for being part of this project and, through his story, hope others will see an opportunity to change a situation they may be experiencing.

— *Dawn*

Knowledge is a combination of information acquired from learning and life experience. Most of what I have to share has come from the latter of the two. Some of what I know now could not have come from a classroom or a book. My life experiences to date have been a culmination of my own endeavors and of others that have crossed my path over the years.

There is an old saying, "A smart man learns from his own mistakes/experiences and a wise man learns from others". In retrospect, growing up I was neither wise nor smart;

however, as an adult I can now say that the knowledge that I possess today is a direct result of many repeated mistakes.

Let me start by saying that my educational experiences are no match for the experiences I have gained through the different life situations I have endured and come to understand. I had to come to a place of willingness and open mindedness in order to gain freedom from the bonds that kept me locked into a meaningless existence.

My journey embarked with the use of alcohol and drugs as an escape from reality. I went through many years of turmoil, confusion and pain until the introduction of a new way of thinking changed the way I perceived life. This changed the quality of my life. I attribute the change to my faith, laughter and humor. My journey took many years, but a simple understanding of bringing back some of my childlike qualities of fun and enjoyment served as some of the greatest tools I have today.

My name is Keith Richard Godwin and I was born in 1967 on Long Island, New York. I was given my first and middle name from my mother who loves me dearly and who had a crush on a famous rock and roll star from the '60s. I was told it was to show mercy on me because my father's name was Benjamin Franklyn Godwin III. My father did not want his son to endure the same ridicule he suffered as a kid like "Ben go fly a kite" and so on. I also have a younger sister that I have been close to throughout most of my life.

My biological father also suffered from addiction during my young adult years. I do not remember him because he was not around when I was a child. He spent the majority of my younger years in prison, and I grew up with someone else filling his role. From what I hear, my father was a decent man with a heart of gold but that drugs and alcohol got the better of him. At some point while in prison he became a minister. He passed away when I was twenty and I wish him peace.

My mother remarried when I was young and my step-father took on the role as "dad". He was not the best father figure you could hope for and was abusive in many ways to my whole family. With me, beatings were a constant thing, and no matter what I did it never seemed to be good enough. My mom came to her senses after a while and he was no longer part of our lives. I was a young teen when he left the picture, good riddance! Unfortunately, a lot of damage was already done. In my efforts to counteract what I was going through at home I became the class clown at a young age. I found that humor helped me to cope with some of the internal struggles I was going through. I am sure everyone reading this has their own family dynamics, and these dynamics may or may not have a direct impact on the choices we make in life. However, neglect and abuse in a family system may cause detrimental consequences in the end. Although I was able to use humor to quiet some of my internal struggles, there were other deep-seated issues that plagued me that I was unable to articulate which kept my life in a downward spiral. In trying to make sense of these issues, and wanting desperately to gain back some control over my life, I turned to abusing alcohol and drugs as an escape from a reality that was my hell at the time. This abuse continued for a good part of my young adult life, and although I felt at some point that I was aware that the way I was living was wrong, I chose to continue down that path.

I barely graduated from high school and after a year of having no direction for my life whatsoever, I decided to join the Marine Corps in 1986. In the Marine Corps my sense of humor was not always appreciated, but I continued to use it to help me to cope. On occasion my sense of humor even got me into a trouble. Consequently, the punishments from my drill sergeant were a lot of pushups, leg lifts and digging in the sand pit. During the four years I was enlisted in the Marines I did "party like a rock star" all over the world. Due to my substance abuse I suffered all the early signs of being an alcoholic: blackouts, fights, even arrests, but I chalked it all up to part of being a Marine. I was not diagnosed as an alcoholic or treated by the military for my problem.

When I was younger I did not know what I know now. When I look back now, because my fun times were centered around my substance abuse, it seemed to me that I was having a good time. But as my addiction increased, the good times decreased. I was fortunate enough to receive an honorable discharge after 4 years of service in the Marines. To this day, being a Marine was one of the things in my life that I am most proud of.

My story from here on is of a life of unmanageability, the same as many other addicts and alcoholics. My circumstances may have been different, but the feelings of hopelessness and despair are the same. I found myself in hospitals, rehabs, and being arrested. I lost my right arm due to being in a car that I flipped over. I was literally being burned alive and I lost all my fingers on my right hand. I feel very blessed to even be alive. I also was stabbed below the heart in a drug buy gone badly. Thank God I am 6 foot 6 inches tall or I would not be writing this today. All that being said, I still continued to use drugs until April 20, 2004 when a 5 foot 1 inch lady who I called "Grammar", my actual grandmother, looked at me and said, "What happen to you, I used to be so proud of you. You were my first born grandchild, a Marine, and now look at you – you are a drunkard!" I felt so low at that point I could have crawled under a rock. Instead, I made a decision that I did not know at the time would change my whole life and my whole way of thinking and living. I told her I was going to get help and I followed it up with an action. I went into a twenty-eight day treatment facility called CK Post. I had the spark I needed to continue in treatment and met others in recovery. This time my ears were wide open. I was so relieved to know I was not alone and that there was help. I was willing to take what was offered to me and to put in the effort to keep it. From this point on using drugs or alcohol would no longer be a part of my story. The healing process was just beginning.

Once I completed the CK Post program, I continued my treatment at the Northport VA where I now work as an addiction counselor. I learned to laugh again while in treatment at

CK Post. I started telling jokes in morning meditation, and I took it upon myself to choose a "Confucius Says" quote daily. Not only did I look forward to doing this every night to bring into the community the next day, but I enjoyed the way I felt when making others laugh. I then realized that the people there looked forward to it, also. One morning when I did not bring a joke or saying everyone was disappointed. It had become something that they looked forward to.

For the first time in my life, in a long time, I was enjoying life without the use of a mood or mind altering substance. I started to make light of my addiction laughing at the idiotic stuff I did. I was even joking with others about my missing hand, and some of the guys gave me a painted rubber glove as a replacement. This was not done in a cruel way. I made light of it, and everyone started to feel more comfortable around me. I began to feel comfortable around myself. I was not treated like a person that was missing a limb but just as a person, and that made me feel like a normal person, which I liked. Laughter helped to empower me over my disabilities. I do not minimize what I had done and what had happened to me. I also do not dwell on it or let it define me as a person.

My recovery continued and my sense of humor was solidified when I saw an opportunity to do comedy at a 12-Step Convention. I decided to go on stage and do some comedy, and for my first time on stage I did pretty well. More importantly, I found I loved doing comedy. The feeling of being on stage and having hundreds of people there laughing was exhilarating. It was then that I made the decision to attend comedy school, and I did very well there, too. I attribute the rest of my story to my addict mentality of getting that next high no matter what, and I just kept moving forward. Comedy was my new drug of choice. I was doing comedy almost every day, and started my own comedy business with a friend I met in comedy class. I have never looked back. I started to take my comedy into 28 day rehabs, crisis centers, and therapeutic communities, and I started working with other comics also in recovery. I thought if laughter worked this well for me, why not bring it to where people needed to laugh the most. This has been going on for the past three years. Together, other recovery comics and I have worked with hundreds of people and have done hundreds of events. We have been doing shows at 12-Step Conventions, for correctional facilities, and on veterans units. We have traveled to different states including New Jersey, Pennsylvania, Virginia and California, all because of the simple concept that laughter heals and increases your quality of life.

The feedback I have been getting from staff and clients alike has been amazing. A staff member once told me that our comedy events make a big difference for their whole day, and that the effects of it sometimes carry over until the next week. I have been told that people count the days until we return for another show. One of the clients told me, "I haven't laughed in years. I really needed that." I have been rewarded in so many ways by sharing laughter that I have started my own humor therapy group where I work. It has become one of the biggest groups at my workplace. Yes, laughter is contagious, and who does not like to laugh?

Everyone in recovery, and most people in life, suffer from some type of guilt, shame and/or remorse. Some people do not even feel worthy of a good time or a laugh. Once we can find the lighter side in something and find humor in something, it empowers us to get over it. I always remind a person that just because we laugh does not mean we are minimizing the seriousness of things that have happened to us or what we have done to others. Laughter just gives us a positive feeling for that moment and then we can build off of that. The words of advice I would have given myself would not have done any good because I was not ready to hear and accept them. Others tried to give me the advice but to no avail. Did I listen? Of course not. Today I wish I did, but then again, my journey is mine and life is full of lessons. I have learned a lot of lessons and I am enjoying life with laughter and a new zest for life. I would like to end this the way I began with the saying, "A smart person learns from his mistakes; a wise person learns from others". If you are struggling with addiction, you can make your decision now. I do encourage laughter and joy to be incorporated into everyone's life. We all have the ability to choose today. I chose laughter and joy over stress and misery.

The disease of addiction does not discriminate. It does not care if you are rich or poor, white, black or yellow, straight or gay. However unmanageable life has become because of substance addiction, there is hope. You have heard my story.

As a counselor I have seen many people who were dealt a hand that was a lot worse than mine. I have seen them go on to be productive members of society in spite of the odds that were seemingly against them.

I hope this helps to paint a picture of a story from hopelessness and misery to hope and joy and to empower you to begin your journey today.

Section 2

Health

"In order to change we must be sick and tired of being sick and tired." ~ Author Unknown

Chapter 13

Graceful Aging Brain

꧁꧂

Contributor: Ruth Curran, MS

*R*uth lives in California. We have talked for hours and hours over the telephone and through email, but have not yet met in person. We were introduced by a mutual friend and our passion to help others have a better quality of life has truly brought us together. Ruth has been dedicated to the Time to Play project with the goal to provide people with resources they need to know so they can enjoy life.

As you know, I have worked in healthcare for many years. When I worked in the skilled nursing facility, one of the things that affected me was the residents who were admitted long term due to Alzheimer's and dementia. It was not the residents that saddened my heart, it was their families. Here they would come day after day, week after week, visit with their loved ones and watch them disappear.

Yes, the illness caused those inflicted with Alzheimer's and dementia a loss of their physical functions as their disease progressed. Some could no longer walk or eat by themselves, and some were "sentenced" to be either in bed or a wheelchair for the rest of their lives. But it was their loss of cognitive capacity that was the worst part. The residents: moms, dads, or siblings, at some point could no longer recognize their family members.

Thankfully, I do not personally have anyone in my direct family affected with these disease processes, but due to what I saw, I did serve a term on the Board of Directors of our local Alzheimer's Association. I participated not with the intention to help "cure" the disease, but with a goal to raise money to create more resources and support for the families. I believe we are all in some way connected and need to support each other.

In my experience I also noticed how many people fear aging. Perhaps this fear is justified, as I believe our society seems to look at "old" people differently. Did you ever stop to think that "those old people" are not burdens, but people with great value and experience that we can and should learn from? That they are people who can help us avoid repeating the same mistakes they made and help us get through life a little easier? After all, that is the purpose of this book!

Other societies respect their elders, and I feel that ours sometimes treats them as burdens and "locks" them away. I personally treasure our seniors and their wealth of information. Do you want to learn things to help make your life easier? Just ask someone.

I will tell you a story that has stuck with and disturbed me for so many years. When I worked at the hospital we had volunteers that were called the "pink ladies". Many of them were retired professionals, and volunteering gave them a passion and a daily purpose. Our specific volunteer was assigned to our office for many years. She performed filing and copying and other clerical tasks to help us out. She actually sat at a little corner of my desk and she used to tell me stories. I was probably twenty years old at the time when she told me how she used to go to New York City on the train every weekend from Long Island to visit her son. When she turned sixty-five years old she was excited. She was now able to get a senior citizen discount! She went to the ticket window (there were no ticket vending machines at that time) to purchase her ticket. When she handed the clerk her driver's license he asked her, "Ma'am, do you need help finding your train or getting on board?" She told me how she could not believe it, that no one had ever asked her that before she became "old". My goodness, how this story stuck with me and caused me to fear becoming older. After all, people just do not look at you the same way as they do when you are younger and "have your whole life in front of you". But, becoming older is not so bad. It is a time of opportunity when you get rid of the "stuff" that has haunted you and when you settle down a bit. We have all heard the expression "Older and wiser", or George Bernard Shaw's expression, "Youth is such a wonderful thing. What a crime to waste it on children". I find these "words of wisdom" to be so true.

Ruth's chapter is a little different than the others. She not only talks about what she has learned, what she now implements in her daily life, and how she developed her passion, but she provides easy to implement things we can do every day to improve our brain health. This chapter is really quite important and intended to be proactive information. I hope you take the time to consider adding or changing up one little thing in your daily routine. Consider it a "no brainer" investment in your future.

— *Dave*

I am a brain game creator, focusing everyday on brain fitness and the ageless brain. I am a proud Baby Boomer who landed, somewhat gracefully, in midlife better than ever. ~ Ruth Curran

I hate to play the "if only game" because I am not sure I would change my path, the path that made me better, stronger, and helped me find my purpose. There are a few "brainy" things, had I known, that just might have been helpful both to me and to those whose lives intertwined with mine. In my contribution to this book, I will share things and observations I have learned and my passion for brain health.

SEE PEOPLE AS PEOPLE, NOT AGES: I am better than I was in my thirties or forties, even in those moments when I cannot find my keys or the exact right word. My peers and contemporaries amaze me daily, even though we all joke about not remembering why we went into a room or not finding our cars in a parking lot. I have learned to see people and not just their age. Here is the part I wish I would have understood long ago. We do not need to "overcome" what comes with age. We need to put all those pieces in per-spective and incorporate them in our current life's mosaic. Each adds color and variety, so why not embrace, celebrate, and use them to maximize the quality of our lives?

In all reality, most of the time we do not need more help just because we are a year older. Often that extra year pro-vides us more to give than a need to take. Respect, dignity, and quality of life should rule how we treat each other, not age.

MISSING A FEW BEATS IS OK: I wish I had known that treating brilliant adults who are temporarily missing a beat, for whatever reason, as if they were children, robs them of their dignity. Struggling to see, hear, or speak, does not make a person less intelligent, *so it is not OK* to dumb it down for someone with a physical or cognitive challenge. I wish I had known to keep it smart and that I understood that I needed to be more patient. I learned that lesson the heart-wrenching way. I watched my brilliant mother struggle with cognitive issues and suffer the indignity of how the world treats people who are temporarily missing a cognitive beat. She had so many rounds of wicked chemotherapy treatments that she sometimes felt the cognitive fog that comes with chemical interventions intended to make us better. We worked together to vanquish the fog, and some days that worked. On the days when she was not quite as sharp, the world did not see the amazing woman who earned a master's degree in the 1950s and stood toe to toe with statesmen, policy makers, and publishers as she fought hard battles against censorship. Respect, dignity, and quality of life should rule how we treat each other, without regard to conditions beyond our control.

BUILD MULTIPLE PATHWAYS: My life experience brought me to where I am now and my quest to provide resources for brain health. The following information is packed with things you can do to help your brain stay healthy and the reasons why you should consider incorporating them in yours, and your loved ones, daily life.

No matter how brain-health conscious we are and how many activities we do to stay on top of maximizing our functioning, things happen along the way – a bump on the head, a stray blood clot, an air bubble moving down the wrong pathway, a momentary lack of oxygen, an aggressive treatment, a disease, a re-routing of a hormone or a neuro-chemical – that use up some of our reserve. I wish I would have known that the brain can be conditioned to be flexible through practice. I could have been practicing what I needed just by fitting a few approaches to problem resolution into my life. Pretty simple — a*ll you have to do is, whenever you can, mix it up, be active, be social, engage your senses, act healthfully, and let go*.

Mix It Up: Our brains crave activity. We actually function better when, every now and then, we confuse things a bit and provide new problems to solve. When you mix things up, you reinforce that there are alternative ways to think, reason, and communicate. Merely rewriting our mental maps opens new pathways and forces us to think differently. That means that if one path is cut off after a bump on the head, the brain knows it can re-route messages and still function. The disruption to life is not as great a way out of the fog, though sometimes in the distance is still within sight.

Brain Exercises You Can Try: **Challenge routines by doing the "usual" in an unexpected way** ▪▪ Button your shirt one-handed; ▪▪ Take a completely different route to the grocery store; ▪▪ Take a hike using a walking stick and switch hands every 5 minutes; ▪▪ Speak Pig Latin; ▪▪ Turn the photos on your desk upside down; ▪▪ Move your menu bar on your computer to the side or top; ▪▪ Eat using your non-dominant hand.

The more you do, the more flexible your thinking becomes, and this flexible thinking then becomes a habit.

Be Active: Your brain needs a good balance of neurochemicals and blood flow to keep everything firing properly.

Physical exercise is **the** best way to nourish your brain and keep that "flow" in balance. Get up and move and the rest will follow.

Working out your brain is not really like working on a muscle group at the gym – you do not technically build mass. However, specific activities like learning new things can be related to increases in both the connections in the brain (the synapses) and the chemicals that feed those connections. An active brain is always building new connections!

<u>Brain Exercises You Can Try</u>: Exercise Your Brain ▪▪ Take a class – in person, online, or via podcasts; ▪▪ Research and plan a trip on-line; ▪▪ Learn a new musical instrument; ▪▪ Master a new gadget (like a smart phone); ▪▪ Start a blog and write posts; ▪▪ Cook either with a recipe or free form – they both challenge you; ▪▪ Take a walk in a nature center and read the signs along the way.

Engage Your Senses*:* You can heighten an experience, create better memory hooks, and create new ways of thinking about that moment by simply engaging your senses more fully. When you enhance experiences from a sensory per-spective, you create new information processing pathways in your brain and increase your brain's processing options.

The much simplified process of experiencing the world looks like this: information comes in through our senses and is sorted and routed, via neural pathways, to the part(s) of the brain that can handle the information best. When you at first see an item (a rose), the associated visual information is sent on that path for processing (this is a perfectly formed, pink rose). Smell it and the information must be sent on a second set of routes for processing. Feel and taste the petal and you have now opened up an entire network of neural pathways. By creating a fuller sensory experience you are feeding those parts of the brain (and those pathways) by keeping them active. However, you are not just sending the information down separate sensory pathways – you are also creating associative pathways. You now have a perfectly formed fragrant, pink rose with silky petals that tastes slightly bitter but floral. From this one experience, you gathered pieces of information that were processed separately through a series of neural pathways and a string of associative information that travelled through a network of pathways as well.

Brain Exercises You Can Try: Engage Your Senses More Fully ▪▪ Change up your cooking with new spices and different textures; ▪▪ Listen to a book or a podcast while working out; ▪▪ Take a sensory walk where you hone in on a different sense each block; ▪▪ Bake bread from scratch; ▪▪ Pair scents with visual and auditory experiences.

Tuning in to your senses will allow you to make new associations and activate multiple parts of the brain while doing something restful and nourishing!

Act Healthfully: When you can, as you can, wherever it fits in your life, do those things that promote good overall health. Your brain is tied to every other part of your body. It must be nourished and kept in proper balance through proper care of all of the other systems in your body. Sometimes that is an easier said than done proposition. I read a blog post by a psychotherapist who said that a multivitamin is "a terrific nutritional insurance". How true. When you cannot get everything your body and brain need through food, find a way to nourish yourself! If you have chronic pain or physical conditions that limit your ability to move, try different types of exercise and do what you can, with your doctor's permission, of course. There are ways to nourish your body's systems no matter your condition.

Be Social: Interacting with others keeps you thinking and engaged in life – in person or online!

Brain Exercises You Can Try: Every Day Ways to Engage with Others ▪▪ Join a book club; ▪▪ Cook with friends and family; ▪▪ Shop at the farmer's market or a specialty store and ask about what you are buying; ▪▪ Play games with others – in person or virtually; ▪▪ Go to the park; ▪▪ Volunteer! ▪▪ Connect with people online through social media or enter a virtual sharing experience.

Let Go: Some days you can have too much of a good thing. Working your brain too hard for too long can simply wear you out. Cognitive fatigue is a real chemical phenomenon that can strike at any time and there is little you can do to stop it.

Yes, our brains want to be active and crave stimulation. There is this interesting idea though, that if we let our minds wander – stop guiding and let go of all structure and control – our brain will find a way to nourish itself. Using functional MRIs, it is possible to see pictures of the brain "at rest". They are surprisingly active and lit up in unexpected ways. Silence the noises and turn off the drive to work quite so hard. Your brain will find those routes that will refresh and renew without having to work at it!

Brain Exercises You Can Try: Let Your Mind Wander
■■Shut out sensory input and take slow deep breaths. Let go by shutting out all things that make your brain overwork and wear it out; ■■ Exercise, fresh air, and music are great restorers as well. Let go by plugging in your ear phones, putting on your walking shoes, and getting some fresh air.

ONGOING QUEST FOR UNDERSTANDING: And then there are the things I continue to learn. Finding the exact right word does not matter. Not being able to pull out the right word every time does not make me any less accomplished or capable or sharp – it just means that my brain may have other ideas about what is important. I am learning to listen to my brain and find those things that truly are more important.

Thanks to the internet (and my smart phone), I do not need to remember everything – I just need to remember how to look things up. That is not lazy or weak, it is just practical.

Humor is both one of the most complicated cognitive tasks and one of the most feel-good processes in the daily human experience. Filling my life with good jokes, funny thoughts, and laughter only serves me well.

Engage in life – play games, talk to people, read, create, sing, dance, learn new things – do what makes you feel good and keeps you active.

And, perhaps the most important — respect, dignity, and quality of life should rule how we treat each other without regard to, well. . . anything.

Chapter 14

Becoming Healthy After Forty Years of Being Unhealthy

৵৽

Contributor: Tami Racaniello, CPFT-HFI

I met Tami a few years ago. She is just a regular person, lovely, friendly and eager to help others. I really became interested in what she had to offer after hearing her story, which will hit so close to home for so many in today's society. Tami experienced a shift in her life. She changed her way of thinking, and her lifestyle, to achieve a 130 pound weight loss. Tami demonstrates to us that there is hope, that we can change and that success is possible.

There are many published articles and statistics on obesity and the increased numbers of those who are affected by lifestyle diseases including heart disease and diabetes. In some way we all know the statistics and what is going on in our communities and family. We all have the ability to learn about a disease process that might affect us or a loved one. We also know, personally, of our struggles to be healthy, our commitment to achieve a healthier lifestyle, and if what we are doing in our own personal lives is pleasing to us or not.

My husband and I discuss diet and exercise all the time. It has been a battle faced by many in our family. One day, he said to me, "You know, being healthy is a full-time job." I thought about that for a while. Recently, it came to me. Yes, being healthy might be a full-time job, ***but what happens if you get fired***? That is really thought provoking, isn't it? If you get "fired" because you are not taking your health seriously, you may become sick, or worse. Your body is your temple. My grandma always told me these wise words, "If you don't have your health, you don't have anything."

Throughout my time working in healthcare I have observed people who have viewed their health in a secondary or in a reactive manner. I used to work with a physician who called it, "finding your religion"; an analogy that illustrated his patients who would start to address their health only after a major health event had occurred. I have many stories of people I talked to after they had experienced a health event and then decided to "start to take care" of themselves, sometimes after damage had already been done. One example is a gentleman I had met that had been a very active volunteer in his community. He had diabetes for many years along with a complication of decreased circulation caused by his diabetes. As a result, two toes on one foot had to be amputated, and the following year he required a below the knee amputation of his other leg due to his disease process. When we spoke he told me, "It's time for me to start taking care of myself." I felt this was a bittersweet discussion. Although I was happy that he was taking an initiative to be healthier, I could not help but wish he had been more proactive before he had gotten to that point. I realize that our bodies are amazing, and that improvements to our health may always remain possible. I also know that starting late is better than never starting to become healthier in our quest for quality of life.

Do I expect our stories to make you automatically healthy? There are no shortcuts out there. The choice is either a temporary band aid or hard work and determination. Like Tami shows in her chapter, *Becoming Healthy After Forty Years of Being Unhealthy*, a lifestyle change can only be adopted when you are ready. What I have learned is that, no matter how many times you tell a person they should do something, they will not implement any type of change unless they **choose** to change.

You will learn how Tami's experiences directed her education and career path, and I thank her for sharing her story and her success. I am grateful to her for providing inspiration that may start others on their path to wellness.

— *Doreen*

From the time I could remember, my grandfather called me "Chubby Checker". At the time I had no idea why, but as I got older I realized it was not exactly a term of endearment.

I was a chubby baby, and with the exception of some growth spurts, a chubby child who became an obese adult. My parents were divorced and I imagine that, as a single parent, my mother did the best she could at the time. However, most of my food came out of cans, packages or bags. As a treat I would look forward to our weekly sandwich and strawberry milkshake at the corner luncheonette. On other days, we would stop just to buy a candy bar. Since my grandparents lived around the corner, I would often go to their house after school where my favorite snacks of cream filled cupcakes and chocolate bars would be waiting in their refrigerator.

My life was filled with contradiction. I ate what I wanted and what I was given, and then I was told I ate too much. It seemed okay to mention or talk about it, but not okay to really do anything about it. Had I come home to find different food available to me, I do not think I would have complained. My upbringing was "children should be seen and not heard", so I was fairly quiet around my family and just would have accepted it. The truth is I do not think my family knew what healthy eating was, how to set portion control, or how to change what they were doing. I remember being brought to doctors about my weight. One basically told my mother, "She has to want to do it, and she needs support." He was a smart man.

When I was with my father, generally once a week, the focus was more on spending time together and less on food, though there was the occasional dessert or ice cream. My dad was an entertainer and concerned about his appearance, so his eating habits were very different then the family I spent the most time with. For reasons not important to this story, I stopped seeing him when I was nine. Had he been in my life as a teenager maybe I would have asked for support, but my life took a different turn.

My mom remarried when I was eight, and my stepdad was a wonderful man. Unfortunately he and my mother both shared the same unhealthy habits. They were smokers, ate processed foods, and were not active. Sometimes we would have dinner at 6 o'clock p.m. and then at 9 or 10 pm they would decide to get a pizza pie as a snack.

I was told to eat less, but the role models I had were doing otherwise. The mantra here was, "Do as I say, not as I do". Though I did smoke socially for a short time, I never really liked it, so it was very easy to give up. Plus, I was starting not to feel well, and a visit or two to the doctor's office was enough to remember why I used to poke my mother's cigarettes full of holes with a pin.

Now that I was getting older, being healthy became a matter of wanting to fit in. I had many friends, boys and girls. I was very personable, but dating was a little different. While I never really found myself without a boyfriend, there were boys who made it very clear that I was not their "type" physically, and I started to get comments from well-meaning family that, "You have such a pretty face, if you'd only lose some weight." From those who thought I was out of earshot I would hear, ". . .if she'd only lose some weight." Some people in school were also not as kind, and then there were the total strangers who felt they needed to make comments. Going clothes shopping was a tortuous experience.

My confusion grew over the contradiction of, "Eat and enjoy, but don't eat, you don't need the calories." My frustration grew by not being taken for who I was, only what I looked like, and having a family who just did not understand their role in any of it led to really poor self esteem. I started "accepting" things in my life. If it was good enough, it was okay. There were times I was very sad, but I hid it well. I was almost always smiling, at least when I was in front of people. My hope when I went out somewhere is that I would not be the fattest person in the room. Yes, I did check. I always let out a sigh of relief if there was someone present who was bigger than me.

I volunteered in my local ambulance squad and became a CPR instructor, an EMT, and an EMT instructor. I went to school to be a lab technician, but never worked as one. Instead I worked in different types of doctor's offices and worked in a hospital, mostly at the front desk. Here I was, for years surrounded by health professionals, educated on the risk factors of many diseases, yet my own health was terrible.

One year after I got married my mother had a stroke. At twenty-eight years of age I became her caregiver. My stepfather's health was already in decline due to heart disease, so I took care of both of them. I made sure the bills were paid, sorted out all their medications for the week, made sure there was food in the house, and drove my mom back and forth to all her doctor appointments. My needs and my health took a back burner.

When I became pregnant with my first child I ate for two. Already obese, I put on more weight and was diagnosed with gestational diabetes. To avoid medication I agreed to see a dietician and check my blood sugar eight times a day. I still gained a significant amount of weight putting me in the high 200s.

Shortly after I had my second child, my mom needed to have surgery because of a gynecological issue. It turned out that the bleeding she was having was due to ovarian and uterine cancer. The surgeon removed what he could, and heavy-duty chemo treatments were scheduled to destroy anything that was left. Running around with my mom, now with two kids, meant I was last in the chain of importance. By this time my stepdad had already passed away, and I was not getting much support in my efforts. My stress level was skyrocketing, and many days I would get frustrated, angry and depressed.

Fast forward to my fortieth birthday and the year I started thinking about my health. I realized I was getting too close in age to when my loved ones had become unwell from illnesses that were preventable through following a healthy diet and exercising. My mom had a stroke when she was fifty-two years old and my stepfather's health problems became life threatening when he was in his early fifties. My sister had diabetes-related health issues and died at the age of forty-five. I decided it was time to eat better and to start to exercise.

Not having any kind of plan, I went on a diet. I tried six different programs, failing at each one. In addition to feeling like a failure, the diet advisors or nutritionists I worked with told me that I must be doing something wrong, because their program was "the best" and worked for everybody. I also joined a gym, and when I asked questions about an exercise, I was shown "the best" way to do it. Another trainer would show me the way I was *supposed* to be doing the exercise, which was not even close to what I had been doing previously, which was already supposed to be "the best" and right way. I did not understand. Why was doing an exercise one way better than another way? Which one was best for me and why? How could I get all this information to make sense?

I put my science and medical background to good use and started to do my own research on food and exercise. What I found was that most people that were "so called" professionals, the people I was looking to for advice, were more about the newest exercises found in the magazines (fads over facts). In the case of the diet programs, those people were only regurgitating the information they were told to say from the company that they worked for.

Wanting to really understand what I needed to be healthy for myself I enrolled in a class to become a personal trainer.

I read every book and went to every lecture I learned about on health and diet. I started to look at food as an ally to better health, not an enemy. The more I learned about exercise the more I grew to love it. I learned to love my body for being strong. I knew what sick felt like, I knew what pain felt like, and I knew what not loving myself felt like. All of those previous diets only reinforced my negative feelings about my body, but now my mindset had changed to a positive thought process.

This was only the beginning of what is now a life quest for me - to seek out and acquire as much knowledge as I can on health, exercise, diet, and wellness. I became a certified personal trainer, fitness, yoga, and pilates instructor and started my own health and wellness business to bring people the right information so they can get healthy. When I work with a client, it is my personal mission to provide them with the most accurate information that I can based on research and facts. I always treat them as an individual, looking at their specific needs and emotional challenges.

Looking back at the pictures of my unhealthy self I know that I will never be in that place again. I know that what other people say has no effect on me. I no longer entertain mixed messages because I can make sense of them. Teaching my clients to own their health and to understand what they need is the best gift I can pass on. In some ways, I wish I knew what I know now when I was younger, but the fact that I went through all I did to learn for myself makes me better at what I do. I am grateful to be able to share my experience and the insight it provided me.

⌒

A little off tangent, but I felt I wanted to expand on something that Tami discussed in her chapter: how hard it may be in this "real world" of business to find people who really do what they say they do. Tami, luckily, was not discouraged in her initial quest to find answers to help her get healthy, but I am sure many people get discouraged after they pay someone for help or they try things that do not work.

How many times have you purchased products or services without achieving results? Luckily, Tami just kept on searching and went on to success. Do not give up when you try something and you do not achieve the results you want. Keep looking until you find what you need. It is out there even though it may take a little work to find the right path.

While working in the healthcare facilities I performed credentialing and obtained verification of education and references for staff privileges. I, as well, earned the title printed on my business card. With Time to Play, I check the credentials of our professionals and know that they have qualifications to be part of this important project to provide resources to others. What I have learned in the "real world" is that anyone can write anything on a business card, and they might not be qualified to do what they say. Time and time again, when I meet people and take their business card,

I have to remind myself that the titles are self-appointed. Tami's account is a reminder that we need to check further into the people who we plan to hire in our personal or business lives.

— Dawn

Chapter 15

Never Give Up Your Search for What Ails You

Contributor: Christie Korth, CHC

*A*s it relates to your health, this chapter really emphasizes why you need to be your own health advocate. I invited Christie to contribute to this book because her story tells us that we need to be persistent in identifying the cause of a health concern. I am sure, if we think about it, we know someone who has had to search for answers as it pertains to health. We know when there is something wrong with our bodies, even if someone says that we are OK. Hopefully, the search story we know was not as extreme as what Christie went through over her twenty years of misdiagnosis before she received a diagnosis of Crohn's Disease.

I, too, had a health search that lasted over twenty years to find the cause of right side abdominal pain, upper right back pain and bloating. I went to a bunch of different doctors and specialists and had lots of blood tests and sonograms. I had pain that would wake me up in the middle of the night and doctors suggested my pain was caused, among other things, by ovarian cysts, scar tissue from having my children, and stress. One doctor wanted to put me on anti-anxiety medications because I was "imagining" the pain, which I refused. I tried yoga to "calm" myself but could not take deep breaths because of my horrible back pain.

After the length of time I suffered I tried to convince myself I was imagining "my illness" and tried to ignore it. It was not possible. I really felt horrible most days, and I felt my symptoms getting progressively worse. My husband thought it was my gallbladder, and worried that it was going to burst one day. Whenever we went away for a vacation, he made a note where the closest hospital was, just in case. I made myself crazy, going through periods of time questioning if it was some type of cancer.

You cannot imagine what it was, and it was so easily cured! By accident I happened upon a news segment where a physician was being interviewed regarding gluten intolerance. I had never even heard the word "gluten" before! I immediately went to the book store and purchased a book. I read the whole thing during that first sitting. <u>EVERY</u> symptom was <u>ME</u>! The abdominal pain, back pain, migraines, bloating, and brain fog. The book suggested eliminating gluten for two weeks to "detox" your body to see if the symptoms went away. I want to just note that I grew up on bagels, pasta and pizza. I cannot recall having a problem when I was younger, and even had lived in Brooklyn, the bagel and pizza Mecca. No one had ever suggested that my symptoms could be due to a food allergy or gluten intolerance. Sure enough, my symptoms disappeared - like magic! I since learned that the wheat we eat today is much different than the wheat we used to eat. There is a lot of information out there on this topic, so feel free to do some research.

A few months later, I happened to "run into" one of the physicians who I had been seeing for weekly treatments. I had not been to his office since my symptoms went away, and he asked how I was feeling. I told him I discovered that the pain was caused, after all these years of suffering needlessly, by a gluten sensitivity. He said something like, "Hmm, could have been," and walked away. *Oh, my goodness!*

Do you think someone, somewhere along the line, could have suggested that food (in this case gluten) may have been the cause? Again, it is so important to be your own health advocate. Not just in finding a diagnosis, but in the direction of care, to assure that you and your loved ones are treated expeditiously and appropriately. If you do not feel well, do not stop searching for a cause. Do not just accept an answer you do not think is right. You know your body best!

Not to make anyone paranoid, but if you do some research, you will find a very large number of medical errors and medication errors that occur every year. I am not going to go into that here, but suggest you look up the Institute of

Medicine and read a bit about medical errors. Be your own health advocate, be safe, and be healthy.

I truly thank Christie for sharing her experience with us so we can learn from her and what she went through. As much as I do not wish her pain on anyone, I do have to note that her experience caused her to pursue an education that has, and will, enable her to help countless others become well.

Christie is a kind and caring person on a quest to educate others. I hope you enjoy her story and the education she has provided.

A quick disclaimer: The following is a recount of Christie's story. She and I talked about "toning down" the dialogue, but decided to leave it this way. It is, after all, her story. It is not intended to insult any physicians or the traditional medical system. We do value our physicians, their many years of training and sacrifice. Christie also added that she is thankful for her physician's help for a plethora of reasons and greatly appreciates modern medicine and its place in society.

— *Dawn*

Our World Today. . . Today, we live in a very strange, complex world. A world where there are more drug commercials on television than any other advertisement combined. By the time our children are in elementary school, they can recite the names of medications, but not the pledge of allegiance. We live in a world that is full of fast food, bearing ingredients that have surely been manufactured by Frankenstein himself. Undoubtedly, our great grandparents would have balked at the "food" we eat today. How is our diet and fast-paced lifestyle affecting us? You can simply check out the number of antacid ads on the television to understand how terribly askew things are. Or you can look at the hard facts.

Digestive disorders plague as many as 60 to 70 million people and render almost 2 million people disabled each year, costing the United States 20 billion dollars in indirect costs[9]. Considering these staggering numbers, it seems that few practitioners are able to resolve digestive problems conventionally. It is my hope to bring awareness regarding our current system of symptom suppression, or the band aid approach, as I prefer to call it. Evidently, we need a new approach, because the present treatment protocols are not working. I should know firsthand, I *used to be* a figure in the above statistical data.

Sadly, as I have learned, many of those with inflammatory bowel disease (IBD) have heard that exact same sentence.

For the first time since 1993, life expectancy in the United States has decreased,[10] and is projected that by 2030 adult obesity rates in some states could rise above 60%.[11]

What kind of horrendous health state is our country in? What has gone so tragically wrong?

While I think that it is fantastic that we have made so many remarkable advances in technology, at the same time, we have strayed away from health advice that our ancestors have always known to be true: eat properly, get enough exercise, and stay away from sweets. These actions that have slipped through the cracks are majorly responsible for the epidemic I see in my private practice today.

It is bittersweet how my phone rings off the hook with people searching for answers and wondering what has gone so terribly wrong with their health. On one hand, I am so blessed to help those that come to see me. On the other hand, the reality of this epidemic is frightening. Digestive disorders are everywhere.

About twenty years ago you never heard a word about IBD or colitis. Most people had never heard the word diverticulitis. But now? Judging by the looks of my booked to the gills appointment calendar, my opinion is that, America, we are in trouble.

My mission as a holistic nutritionist is to help those with digestive ailments overcome them. Through my own harrowing life experience battling Crohn's disease, my calling in life was born. By harnessing the power of nutrition and a healthful lifestyle, I now live symptom free and know that others could, as well. I am walking, breathing, living proof that you CAN reverse the effects of this disease and leave them behind you. I know many experts will disagree with me and say that Crohn's is not a reversible illness. That is true, but you can most certainly live your days pain and symptom free.

How? Start asking questions about your illness. Be proactive. Look at your relationship with food. This is the first step to living symptom free. Most of those with Crohn's have done their fair share of asking questions and have come up with little or no answers. The goal of me telling my story is to share with you what I know now that I wish I knew then. My goal is to provide you with options and soothe you when your doctor tells you,"Your digestive issues have nothing to do with your food. You can happily eat whatever you want," and before you can protest, your physician then proceeds to quickly shoe you out of the office with a stack of prescriptions.

Sadly, as I have learned, many of those with irritable bowel disease (IBD) have heard that exact same sentence.

At the time my doctor informed me that my digestion was completely separate from my relationship to my food, I had not yet received any formal biological or nutritional education. Yet, I did not feel comfortable with his explanation. It made me crazy! **How could what I eat have *nothing* to do with my digestion?** I later learned that the answer my doctor gave me was <u>so</u> wrong! **<u>You are what you eat!</u>**

When the doors of the medical world are slammed in your face, one by one, until there are no more to open, you come to a realization. I am on my own with this. That is why I wrote this chapter, so you know that you are not alone.

I am going to explain what I learned from my experience how Crohn's Disease affects you physically and emotionally, positive ways to control your illness, and how you can benefit tremendously from self-growth and awareness to enjoy optimum health.

My goal is to let you know that if you have IBD, I understand you and I want nothing more in this life than to give you information so you can get better. You, too, can hop off the Crohn's Roller Coaster for good and learn how to keep your body in remission with the foods that you eat.

Are you ready?

Life with my Unpredictable Belly: My intestines and I, we are forever bonded in a way that most will never quite understand. We have been through a lot together, to say the least. In the end, we were almost separated for good. People told me I was stupid or downright crazy for arguing with my doctors about removing my nutrition starved, terribly damaged intestines, but I refused to fold. I came into this world with them, and I refused to leave without them.

From the time I was nine, my poor mother had dragged me from doctor to doctor trying to uncover the root cause of my mysterious stomach ailments. Each doctor had something to say, but had never provided the correct answer to my problems. Many people who suffer from IBD receive numerous incorrect diagnoses before they reach the right one. Let us start off with some of my funky diagnoses during the first nineteen years of my life that I encountered:

Misdiagnosis Diagnosis # 1: "She has dairy intolerance, she will grow out of it," my pediatrician preached. With all of my test results coming back within normal parameters, the doctor was stumped. She figured dairy must have been the cause of my stomach issues because, evidently, she could not think of anything else. So, it was onto Lactaid milk and days without the ice cream man, but if it cleared up my tummy problems, heck, I was game! After my Mom and I realized that eliminating dairy out of my diet did not seem to change my symptoms, it was back to whole milk and my ice cream treats.

Misdiagnosis Diagnosis # 2: "She needs to be on Zantac and Mylanta for her to digest food properly," remarked the pediatric gastroenterologist. I did not care for that regime. On a fifth grade class field trip to the Natural History Museum, my bottle of Zantac leaked all over my brand new outfit, forcing me to be stained purple and smell like feet all day. From that point on, my classmates would forever dub me as the "sick girl". Hell, I knew me as the sick girl. I spent half of that bus trip in the bathroom. My teacher, who I adored, looked at me with such pity while assessing the damage of my now purple attire.

It was the first time I remember knowing that something was really wrong with me. I was not like everyone else. It was not enough that I could comprehend what the word "endoscopy" meant, or that I had experienced this torturous test without anesthesia, or that I practically lived in my doctor's office. It was that day, when she looked at me, that

I knew something was off. Then she asked me the kicker question, "Is this medicine helping you?" That really got me thinking after my third trip to the bathroom that hour. "No, Mrs. C, I guess it's not."

Misdiagnosis Diagnosis # 3: "She has intestinal flu," **an ER doctor told my mother and I, "Admit her right** **away!"** This diagnosis came when I landed myself in the hospital for close to two weeks from vomiting and diarrhea. I had lost twenty pounds in two days.

I was only eleven at that time and I will still never forget how I spent those days withering in pain. It was during that "adventure" at the hospital when I learned how to laugh even at my worst health. Humor was now my vehicle for coping with everything. It was also a pivotal moment for me, looking back now, as I am certain this was my very first serious flare up of my Crohn's Disease.

I went on like this for eight more years, intermittently sick and well. I was still in and out of the doctor's office, still pooping like it was going out of style, and still missing out on birthdays and school because of my out of control digestion. Because a doctor had not made a diagnosis, it was assumed that I was fine and just had a "sensitive stomach".

Bravely, I trudged through my teenage years and endured everything from acne to depression, from addiction to bloody stools. You name it, I had it. By the time I started ninth grade, I was beyond tired and it showed. I had horrible dark circles under my eyes and I was always exhausted. I could not understand why I could not keep up with anyone or anything. Eventually I started blaming myself. I was an honor student and an over-achiever. I became increasingly frustrated with my lack of ability to keep up with life.

To boot, my relationship with my family had become strained. Both my mother and father thought my mysterious stomach dilemma had all manifested in my head. This brought me to the next set of doctors.

Misdiagnosis Diagnosis # 4: "You have 10 heads and 8 of them are not screwed on straight." This ridiculous and extraordinarily unprofessional diagnosis came from a psychiatrist who dismissed my agitation over my illness and symptoms as "a way to receive attention". Needless to say, my mother practically dragged me out of that guy's office before she strangled him for being so rude.

Misdiagnosis Diagnosis # 5: "You have mono." I was sixteen and my doctor had read me that "death sentence". "What?" I thought. I had been falling asleep in between my incessant bathroom breaks at school and had chalked my sleepy symptoms to that. Or there was also the possibility I had been bitten by some rare sleep inducing bug who was out to plague me. The mono diagnosis entitled me to a "get out of school free" card. I was home schooled for my entire tenth grade year. I missed my friends and my life and I desperately wanted *out;* out of this abyss of never-ending illness.

The summer of my tenth grade year, my stomach became much worse. I was dealing with a lot of stress at home, my parents had discovered my smoking marijuana to ease my stomach pains and were not happy about it at all, as you can imagine. Coming from a family who was entrenched in addiction, they were determined that I did not wind up a "useless addict". I was forced into an inpatient rehab facility. I hardly ate the whole time I was there because I knew that without the marijuana, I could barely eat without vomiting. It was then that a lovely social worker who was missing her top lip suggested:

Misdiagnosis Diagnosis # 6: "You have an eating disorder." I was sentenced to attend a mandatory eating disorder group. When I began talking about my love for ice cream and bread and cookies and pasta, the other women in the group looked at me as if I had landed from Mars.

One young lady said, "What the hell are YOU doing in here?" I looked at her quizzically and said, "If someone can answer that question, I would be really happy." With that, I got up and walked out. The social worker who was missing her top lip no longer forced me into that group after that altercation. Instead, I was sent to 12-Step meetings with other teens. Eventually, someone was bright enough to realize that I did not have a drug problem, but was suffering from a lot of physical pain and I was discharged.

It was at this point that I had given up on ever receiving a diagnosis, and just decided to trudge on, life as usual. It was certainly better than being told I was crazy, or that there was nothing wrong. My solution became ignorance. Ignorance is bliss, right? Well, maybe not.

When You Cannot Ignore Your Body Anymore: In the fall of 2001, I was enrolled in college and doing very well. All in all, things were pretty good. But one fateful day, things started to change. I was sitting at work one morning, alone, when I got a shooting pain in my stomach and became frightened. The pain was so intense I fell down to the floor landing in the fetal position. Confused and scared, I crawled into the bathroom. I was shocked at what I saw. I swore I was bleeding internally.

Instead of calling a doctor, like a normal person would do, I decided it was best to ignore this problem. Remember, I truly believed that living my life with my messy tummy was normal, because no one at this point was able to tell me otherwise. The bloody toilet episodes continued and then became more and more frequent.

It was at that point that I could not deny something was up any longer. I had dropped from a healthy 130 lbs to 110. My ribs were poking out of my body and if I bent over, you could view the entire outline of my spine. Fellow students would gawk at me, complementing me on my weight, making remarks like "You are so skinny, you lucky girl."

"Yeah right," I would retort sullenly.

For every person who admired my new illness ridden body, there were those who were very concerned about my non-fashionable skeletal appearance. Friends had begun asking me if I was snorting cocaine or if I was anorexic. Even my social work professor had made a comment after a class asking me if I was all right.

The icing on the cake came while I was at a party with my friends one evening. We were eating dinner when suddenly I was plagued by that sharp, stabbing pain. It washed over me like a tidal wave. I fell on the floor and vomited again and again and again. My friends looked on and tried to help, but all anyone could do was watch me vomit helplessly and hold my hair back. The final time I vomited it was straight blood.

It was that night at my friend's party when his mother looked at me and said, "Honey, I think you need a hospital." I knew something was very wrong.

Does Anyone Have A Clue? I woke up in the Recovery room, groggy and out of sorts. I had just had a colonoscopy to determine the cause of my relentless stomach issues. A nurse optimistically walked past me and smiled, "How are you doing, my dear?" I gave her a half smile and a thumbs up. "Are you up for company?" I nodded.

My doctor walked in and looked at me with pity.

"Christie, you have something called Crohn's Disease."

And just for a split second, the whole world stopped for me. My thoughts were racing. I pictured every single doctor who had told me that absolutely nothing was wrong with me. I went through every day of pain, suffering and scariness and felt the instantaneous relief of validation.

"I am writing you out a prescription and leaving it at the desk. You need to follow up with me next week." And with that, he left before I could even ask him anything. I was utterly in shock at this point. I did not think I could have even asked him a question. I was literally dumbfounded. After nineteen years, I knew. I thought I was good to go. Take some pills, move on, live life. Well, not quite. . .

Just Take Some Pills and It Will Go Away? In December 2003, right before Christmas, I landed myself a "vacation" from work. Despite the litany of medications I had tried, nothing had seemed to work. In fact, I was just getting worse and worse. I spent a week in the hospital, hallucinating on morphine and listening to nurses uttering encouraging phrases like, "I don't know if that girl is going to make it." I was on enough steroids for puny little me to lift a building, yet I was weaker than my kitten Precious. I felt like I had run through a tornado and it had torn my stomach in half. The doctor was considering removing part of my small intestines, which were beyond inflamed. One of the nurses read my CT scans and had commented, "I have never seen intestines like *that.*" The surgeon came in and felt that if I did not have my intestines removed, I would die.

Now, I told you that I was stubborn. My family and friends begged me, but I refused the operation with all my power. I knew that I would make it out of there with my body intact.

I Saw the Sign: Somehow, the inflammation in my intestines reduced over the following week. After two weeks on every medication know to man, I was released from the hospital, intestines intact. The following day, I would start outpatient therapy on a drug called Remicade, which is essentially compromised of mouse antibodies. I was reluctant to start this therapy. I joked that I would turn into a mouse and dreaded dealing with it. Remicade was the end of the line for me. If this did not work, I would have no other choice but to let my surgeon remove my intestines.

As it turned out, I was allergic to the Remicade, so instead of going off it and then be forced into surgery or chemo, I was given Benadryl to counteract my hives and other side effects. One day after starting my infusion and succumbing to one of my hypnotic Benadryl states, I overheard the woman next to me talking about Crohn's Disease. In my sleepy stupor, I heard her mention a book she read about Crohn's Disease and how this book had *saved a friend's life*. My ears perked up like those of a blood hound.

It took every ounce of my energy to open my eyes and look at this woman. "I have Crohn's Disease too," I mumbled. She looked up at me and said, "Honey, you look like you need some rest. I will write down the name of this book for you. You can read it and you will get better."

With that, this angelic woman hastily scribbled down the title and author and handed it over. She claimed this book had saved a dear friend of hers who had been suffering with Crohn's. She grabbed my hand gently and whispered, "You are going to make it past this, sweetheart."

I was baffled by the whole experience. Initially, I thought this woman had lost her marbles and I obviously was no better being in my strange drunken Benadryl state. I closed my eyes, half expecting the paper with the name of the book would not be there when I awoke from what must have been a demented dream.

After the Bendryl wore off and my infusion was almost over, I woke up to Carol the nurse, humming cheerfully, "Hello, sleeping beauty, your lunch is here!" I shook myself awake, eyeing the tray of food, debating whether to eat it or not. Suddenly, I remembered the crazy dream I had had. "Wait a minute," I thought. Maybe. . . I looked in my pocketbook. "I'll be damned," I stammered out loud. In my chocolate brown handbag, written in chicken scratch, were the words: *Patient Heal Thyself* by Jordan Rubin. Then written below that was, "You're going to make it sweetie! Good Luck!"

If that was not my sign from above, then I was foolish. I did not waste a moment. Carol came over and unleashed me from my IV pole. I ran out of the infusion center like a bat out of hell and drove as fast as I could to one of my favorite places, the library. I left the library discouraged. They did not carry Jordan's book. On a whim, I decided to visit the bookstore. At the very least, they could order me a copy.

I browsed around the titles, inhaling the sweet smell of the new books. I discovered the health section and scoured the shelf for books on digestive wellness. Again, I did not see Jordan's book. I began to think that the woman from the hospital was nuts and there was no such book.

Just as I was ready to leave the aisle, a woman brushed past me and put a book back on the shelf. I was crouched down, scrambling down the list of titles on the bottom shelf to ensure I had not missed anything, when I was literally attacked by a book. I looked up and had to laugh as the book the woman put back came crashing down on my head. I was a little annoyed until I looked down at the book. I dropped it and gasped, "Jesus, Mary and Joseph. . . ." Staring me in the face were the words "Patient Heal Thyself."

A New Beginning: I went home and read *Patient Heal Thyself* from cover to cover. Jordan's book focused on eating foods from the Bible. This seemed logical to me, despite the fact I was not the most religious person at that time. For some reason, my gut instinct told me that this had to help. I diligently started his diet.

A major breakthrough was coming to terms with the fact that all of the food I had been eating was pure garbage. I was out running to the border and having midnight taco festivals in between my college, party and work schedule. No more of that!

It was on to learn about organic foods and to try many new foods that were foreign to me. Fortunately, my boyfriend was a produce manager and extremely well schooled in the "University of Organics". Besides that, he was a fantastic cook and willing to help. I felt a special bond with my favorite cook, Rachel Ray who taught me how to eat real food. I had grown up on a diet of meat and potatoes without fresh vegetables. My childhood diet had also included a lot of processed foods like white bread, cookies, rolls and cakes. Cereal had been a huge staple food for me. I could eat any type of cereal by the truck load. Cereal was forbidden on my new diet, but I found new favorite foods. I increased my intake of fruits and vegetables, all the while falling in love with cooking and experimenting. I also started a regime of supplements including probiotics and digestive enzymes.

A couple of weeks into starting the diet and taking the supplements, I started to notice that I actually had energy. Then, it hit me. I woke up one morning and did not have pain in my stomach. At first, honestly, I thought I was dead. In all the years, for as long as I could remember, I woke up dealing with stomach pain. But, that morning in early 2005, it was gone. . . vanished.

I jumped out of bed and called everyone I knew. I wanted to tell everyone and anyone who would listen that I had gotten myself well. My doctor did not seem impressed, in fact, he was dismal. "You know Christie, you should make sure you continue taking the Remicade, it's a good drug." My blood was boiling. If I heard the words one more time, "It's a good drug," surely I would scream. How could he dismiss all of this, I wondered.

I started to radically change the way I thought. I studied Crohn's Disease, food, politics, and nutrition. When telling friends about my story, I was always told how incredible it was. I was doing better and better each day. As long as I took the probiotics and ate well, I was fine. I even started going to the gym regularly, and I began to gain some of my weight back. Eventually, I became so enthusiastic I decided to change my major from social work to nutrition.

The Culprit that Caused it ALL! In the fall of 2006, it was then that I went on to discover the root cause of my illness: BREAD! I had begun to experience some symptoms again, and a classmate suggested I have my DNA tested for gluten intolerance.

I told her that, when I was younger, I had been tested for Celiac Disease and it had come back negative. She looked and me and said boldly, "That doesn't matter, honey, maybe you are intolerant to gluten. That type of allergy is different. Just check it out, you have nothing to lose." She was right.

I went home that evening and searched on the internet for a lab that could test me for a gluten allergy. I found one and was impressed. I was overjoyed to know I might be closer to learning what may be wrong, and decided to order the DNA testing right away; after all, I had nothing to lose.

Bread was Killing Me: It was Valentine's Day, February 14, 2007, at 6:00 a.m. when I received an email from the lab. I had been up every day at the crack of dawn, checking for my test results. I was patient. I had waited, and now they were here. I was almost afraid to look at the results. I opened the email and scanned down the page, and then I read:

You possess two copies of a gene, one from your mother and one from your father that predisposes you to gluten intolerance, which is considered severe. In order to preserve your health and prevent further damage, it is highly recommended that you strictly adhere to a gluten free diet for life. It is indefinite that your children will possess at least one copy of the gene, and should remain gluten free, as well.

I got halfway down the page and I had to stop reading. The tears were flowing so fast that I was unable to see the computer screen. In that moment, never have I been so grateful. I dropped down to my knees and thanked God from the highest place in my heart. It was over.

After twenty-four years of living life in fear of the next sick moment, I now knew what was causing it the whole time: bread. Damn bread. Here I was, an Italian that grew up on bread, only to discover it was killing her. It was crazy. I started calling every single person I knew to tell them I was going to get better.

That, I did. Six months after totally going gluten-free, my stomach was like a tank, solid and strong. As long as I was gluten-free, I could eat almost anything. My blood work looked perfect, better than it ever had. My energy and stamina improved, and for the first time in my life, my acne cleared up. I could not have been happier. On the day of my college graduation, I was prepared to begin my mission. Going through this ordeal had changed my life in so many ways. I now knew my disease was a blessing. It taught me to never give up hope and to always trust your instincts. I am thankful, most of all, that it created what is now my livelihood. I cannot picture doing anything else in this life except helping people get well. I am a healer. I know it had always been God's plan for my life.

A new chapter in my life had begun, and I am on a mission to help as many people with IBD as possible. I want nothing more than to make sure they all know they are not alone, and that there is hope for them to live well. I am living, breathing, and walking proof of what can happen when you find healing. Today, I am off all medications for Crohn's and

I only flare if I go off my diet of get too stressed. To find a way to cope with this disease has been a godsend and I am forever grateful. I am now on a mission to help as many people with Crohn's and Colitis as possible.

I hope my story has inspired you. If you know something is wrong, keep pursuing. Be an advocate for your own health and the health of your loved ones. Here's to your health.

Chapter 16

An Illness Does Not Have to Stop You from Living Life

ᕙᕐᕗ

Contributor: Jean Rose Castiglione, RN

*J*ean Rose, lovingly known to many as JR, was one of the first people I talked to about the idea for this book in 2004. JR is a Registered Nurse and was the Nurse Unit Manager at the nursing home where I worked at the time. When I saw her a few months ago, she asked me, "So, when are we writing this book?" It was finally the right time. I credit JR with actually pushing me to get this project going.

JR is an inspiration. As a nurse, she has cared for those sick and frail for forty years, making sure all their needs are met. She is kind and compassionate and very strong. She has dealt with her own chronic illness since 2003, which she explains in her chapter, but has not let it stop her from living her life or enjoying her life.

Working in healthcare for over twenty six years myself, you see two types of people. Some will get a diagnosis and decide that is it and give up, while some will get a diagnosis and will not let it beat them. We have all heard the miracle stories, after the doctors say someone will "never come out of it" they wake up, or those that are told will "never walk again" not only walk, but run.

JR shows that there is no finality to a diagnosis, and that it does not have to hamper daily life or quality of life. She is truly an inspiration to others, to her patients and their families. She is a lover of life and a friend to all.

Additionally, there are the stories of people who "disappear" when there is an illness or other disruption in a friend or family member's life. Maybe we have been the one who has "disappeared". It may be that we do not know how to deal with or how to approach a situation, but perhaps that is when they need us the most. JR's discussion about compassion and our support of others who need us is something that should be greatly considered. However, I have recognized that loyalty in our society may be decreasing. We see evidence of this everyday in comparison shopping and looking for the cheaper price instead of buying at the place we have patronized for years. We also see this in our workplace with decreased job security. Perhaps we should reconsider the benefits of a loyal employee or loyal service. Loyalty is a value we should cherish. It is a lesson we should pass on to our children. Perhaps embracing loyalty and compassion would make our world just a little better, a little less stressful, and a little more enjoyable.

I thank JR for sharing her story, and I know that she will be there to help others through their illnesses and struggles for many more years to come.

— *Doreen*

August 2003 was a month filled with happiness. I was planning both my daughter's sweet sixteen and mother-in-law's seventieth surprise birthday party.

The day before my mother-in-law's party was a Friday, and I went to my gynecologist for a routine exam. While palpating my abdomen the Nurse Practitioner "felt something". She wanted me to come in the next day for a sonogram. I told her the earliest I could come in was Monday, as my mother-in-law's party was on Sunday and I had so much to do.

On Sunday night, after the party, I had a feeling of uneasiness and I started to wonder why the Nurse Practitioner wanted me to have the sonogram the next day, which was a Saturday. I pushed it out of my mind since I was going for the test the following day, which was Monday.

Early Monday I went to the doctor's office and while having the sonogram, the technician excused herself and left the room to "get the doctor". The doctor came in, reviewed the sonogram, palpated my abdomen, and immediately told me that there was a "mass" and he wanted me to go for blood work as soon as I left his office.

I could not get into my car fast enough to call my husband and tried to explain to him what occurred in between sobs. That August, at the age of 48, my life was going to make a drastic change and move into another direction.

On September 30th, I had a complete hysterectomy with debulking (cleaning out). I was diagnosed with ovarian cancer, stage 3. I started chemotherapy in November after having a med-a-port inserted to make chemotherapy access easier, since my veins may not be cooperative.

Prior to starting chemotherapy, my husband buzzed my head. I looked as though I belonged in the military. I went wig shopping. I remember crying the first time I put on the wig, but I adjusted to wearing wigs and never having to have a bad hair day! There are so many lovely styles available and quite frequently people complimented me on my "hairstyle" and asked me who does my hair!!

As a Registered Nurse I was always diligent with getting pap smears, mammographies and going to the doctor. I did not feel I neglected myself, in fact I felt the opposite and that I was on top of everything. Ovarian cancer cannot be detected by a pap smear, and to my knowledge none of my relatives had ever had this type of cancer.

There are not any early symptoms. This is why ovarian cancer is known as the "silent killer". By the time symptoms occur, the cancer has spread. Symptoms include bloating, gassiness, vaginal bleeding (which I did not have), back pain, bowel changes, and frequent urination. I had experienced bloating, gassiness and frequent urination (I drink lots of water) symptoms since the start of my menses at age 13.

I always felt, as a nurse, that I never had to experience an illness to have compassion and empathy for my patients. I felt fortunate because there were many times since being diagnosed that a patient would be in my care that had a "history of ovarian cancer", and I was able to see that they were well into their sixties or seventies. I felt that God sent this person to me to give me strength, inspiration and hope.

When I was diagnosed, I decided to be involved in a study program. I chose a very aggressive treatment which included three chemos. I also chose to work during my treatments and would schedule them on Thursdays or Fridays to give me the weekend to "recuperate". I found working therapeutic. I was concerned that not working would give me more time to "dwell on my problem", and I knew having a positive attitude was extremely important. Many nights, past and present, I am too tired to think of anything but sleep when I get home!

I was cancer free from 2003 to 2008. In September 2008, I had a reoccurrence of cancer which required another surgery to "debulk" (clean out) it with chemo to follow.

At present, I am currently receiving chemo, working full-time and enjoying life. I firmly feel that cancer is a "chronic" disease, comparable to hypertension, diabetes, heart disease, etc. Since being diagnosed I have had to step back and re-evaluate my relationships. I am not a "doom and gloom" person and choose to be optimistic and have a positive attitude. I also make it a point to surround myself with positive and happy people. I have wonderful doctors who are dedicated, supportive, and knowledgeable and are at the top of their field. I tried attending support groups, but the meetings interfered with my hectic work schedule.

Early on, when I was first diagnosed in 2003, I had to choose a different doctor because he was extremely negative and told me that my prognosis was not good. I cannot imagine doing as well as I am if I had continued to be his patient!

For me, not working was never an option. I wanted to get back to what my life was like "before I had cancer". Even though my diagnosis brought challenges, the most disheartening challenges I have encountered is from my own profession. I am considered a "liability" because of my history of cancer and employers are hesitant to offer employment to someone like myself. I am under my husband's health insurance because of this. I have had perfect attendance and do not call in sick. In fact, I am lucky enough to get paid out for my sick time at the end of every year! I resent being treated this way and I feel as though I am punished for having this chronic illness when others abuse their time/attendance benefits. At one time, all I had to do was send my resume out and I would get many calls for interviews and have job options to choose from.

So many people, young and old, continue to deal with daily struggles and challenges. Imagine if we all turned our backs on them. We say we are dedicated, compassionate and empathetic, but yet when we have the opportunity to prove that we truly are, we walk away.

After reading this, what will you choose to do the next time you are approached by someone who needs your support?

Section 3

Finance / Work Life Balance

ﻌﻌﻌ

"Don't let life discourage you; everyone who got where he is had to begin where he was" ~ Richard Evans

Chapter 17

Learning to Make My Money Work

꧁꧂

Contributor: Laurence Dresner, ChFC, RTRP

*W*hen Larry and I met he believed in my idea to provide resources to others so they can learn what they need in order to enjoy life. After hearing his story, I realize it was because he had to learn what he needed to know on his own. His story tells how he approached others for assistance in his financial success and they did not "give him the time of day".

In many instances, I have observed so many people be reactive in their lives. Many of us do not look into things we might need to know unless we have no choice. Sometimes it is too late and we are unprepared for a situation. I believe it is best to at least be familiar with a variety of topics in the event a situation arises. No, we cannot know everything about everything, but in my opinion it is better to know a little about something.

I will give you an example. Many people today are in a "sandwich generation" situation. In my time working in a skilled nursing facility (nursing home), many people came in to the admissions department not knowing what to do with mom or dad, that they no longer could live alone or needed physical rehabilitation after an illness or injury. Unfortunately, there had been no pre-planning. Their parent had no way to pay for care, and the family could not figure out how to pay for the care they needed. People sat across from me at the conference table and cried. It was a truly heartbreaking situation. What do I suggest? A little pre-planning for things we know may be coming down the pike. If you have kids, they may need to go to college someday. If you have parents, they may need medical care, or you might, too. Do you have a will? Do you have a healthcare proxy? Just some things you may want to consider. I believe it is better to think about them now, when not in a crisis situation, then to have to figure things out in an emergency.

In Larry's situation, no one wanted to help him work with investments because he did not have much to invest. He talks about his journey to learn and to grow, as well as his quest to help others who need help planning for their future. "I don't need money", you might say. I beg to differ. Through my journey in Time to Play and my "quest for quality of life" I have learned that we do need money. As a matter of fact, it is our responsibility to make a lot of money so we can donate to others: food banks, churches, etc., to help them. I realize that, if we do not have money, we cannot help other people. I used to be embarrassed asking for money or charging for my services. I now realize that I was not only hurting myself, but I was hurting others.

We all may have grown up with preconceived ideas about money, and I know I did. I grew up believing rich people were "bad", and asking what in the world people could have done to get that house, that car, etc., which I have covered in my chapter *Digging Deeper*. I now know that this incorrect programming hurt me in my life, and hampered me from helping others. A friend recommended a great book, *Money is My Friend* by Phil Laut. I suggest you read it if you think money is bad, as it will help you find out why and to break free from the negative thinking that holds us back.

I thank Larry for sharing the information on how he made his money work for him, and hope it can get you on the road to seeking ways to get your money, no matter how little you have to start with, to work for you. I do want to note that the opinions expressed about the investment industry are those of the chapter author and are in no way meant to be slanderous. The goal of this chapter is to make people think and be more aware to do the right things for themselves. After all, we are all in this together.

— Dawn

I was twenty-five, newly married and clueless about finance. Sure, I worked small jobs as a kid growing up including a newspaper delivery boy, caddy, and I even spent some time as a short order cook in a bar, but that was all for spending money and fun. I put very little into savings. In fact, the only money I saved was so that I could buy things without my parents knowing about it – enough said.

My parents paid for college and I knew I had student loans, whatever that was, for graduate school. But none of this prepares you for paying bills, balancing a check book, prioritizing purchases, etc. I would receive almost weekly calls from penny stock brokers wanting to sell me investments, most of which I did not understand. In hindsight, it is a good thing I did not invest in them. But, when I approached investment companies needing help with my meager savings, without fail, they rejected me because my net worth was too small for them to bother with. The ones I called upon were all going after the "big fish", which, back then were people with investable assets of $100,000 or more. That really made me angry. Just because I did not have the big bucks, I still needed to make what money I did have work for me. That is when I started on a quest to teach myself how to invest. I read *Money* and *Forbes Magazine* and the *Wall Street Journal,* and it was the best education I could have hoped for.

The more I learned, the more I realized how self-serving the broker/dealers were when it came to recommending products that are *supposed to be* for the benefit of the investor. They touted real estate partnerships, penny stocks, and more, all to make a fat commission or win a sales competition at their branch. So much of the industry's literature was geared to making people believe that you can beat the market if you used their research and services or that their products would solve all your financial concerns. However, the empirical research by independent colleges and universities consistently poked holes in this belief. The more I learned, the more I was determined not to fall prey to all their financial pornography. When I decided to become a financial planner, I promised myself that I would accept any client, regardless of their net worth. My only criteria in accepting someone was that they had to be sincere in wanting to take control of their finances. My fees are based on services and advice, not product commissions, so that there is less conflict of interest. Because of this I knew I would never survive in a broker/ dealer environment that requires reaching benchmarks of sales and commissions or getting fired, so I went independent. My more consultative approach took a much longer time for me to become profitable, but at least I knew I was doing right by my clients.

In today's environment, the financial services industry is more heavily regulated, and companies and brokers are much better at not recommending inappropriate products to customers, but there still is room for improvement. I have found that most companies, with the exception of a few, still ignore the middle class investor because it is not profitable.

There is so much debate between term and whole life insurance. I have seen the benefit for a widow receiving the cash balance from a whole life insurance policy which made a difference for her that a term life insurance policy would not have provided. I have given up a lot in commissions over the years by recommending term insurance because it was the right choice for a particular situation rather than try to sell whole life. I have seen the benefit of estate planning for one family versus the chaos and hard feelings for another family that insisted they did not need estate planning. I have seen the smile of gratitude from parents who were able to help their kids pay for college. I have received thanks from people who I helped save money, even though I did not make any. But my client's appreciation is what makes it all worthwhile. I have also experienced the frustration from people refusing to take action even when my recommendations are clearly appropriate and beneficial to them. I have felt despair from educating clients just to see them make the same mistake again. I have come to learn that I can only do so much, and as long as I feel that I did the best possible to help them, what they ultimately choose to do is out of my control.

For most people, money is a means to an end, not an end in itself. The end would be a comfortable retirement, a vacation home, yearly travel, children's education, etc. But there never seems to be enough money to go around. How do you prioritize your "ends" or goals so that you feel good about your choices while still accomplishing what you set out to do?

Everyone will have their personal opinions about how important money is and whether money will make them happy. A financial advisor, George Kinder, asks his clients these three questions: 1) If you have enough money to take care of your needs, now and in the future, how would you live your life? Would you change anything? 2) Your doctor says you have only five to ten years to live. You will not feel sick, but you will never know when death will come. What will you do? Will you change your life? How? 3) If your doctor says you have only one day left to live, ask yourself: What did I miss? What did I not get to be or do?[12] These are extremely powerful questions, and really get to the root of a person's beliefs and attitudes about money.

Many advisors advocate that a person set up individual accounts, or "buckets", for each of their goals based on the time horizon of when they need the money. Short term buckets can include monthly living expenses such as rent/ mortgage, loan payments, groceries, a yearly vacation, etc. A mid-term bucket might include saving for a home purchase, or a child's education. A long-term bucket would be retire- ment savings, or a vacation home purchase. Each bucket requires a different approach to investing.

Author Lee Eisenberg wrote a very popular book, *The Number – A Completely Different Way to Think About the Rest of Your Life*. It goes beyond mere numbers and demo- graphics. It forces you to rethink how you will live the last third of your life and makes you answer questions that will help shape the quality of your life during retirement.

Financial planning is not just about numbers. It is also about hopes and dreams. Hope that you can adequately provide for your family. Hope that your children will be happy, healthy and have financially secure lives. Dreams about leaving a lasting legacy for your heirs. One way to do that is what I recommend to my clients, by creating a personal legacy statement.

A personal legacy statement is a document that you would write or record on video about yourself for future family members to read and share. Consider your personal legacy statement as a way to pass information and family stories along to future members. You can talk about your dreams and ambitions, challenges that you overcame, stories of particular importance to you about yourself and/or family members (spouse, children, pets, etc.). Write what growing up as a child was like. Describe your parents, siblings, childhood friends, teachers and other family members. Reminisce about how life today is different than life was as you were growing up. It is a way to describe you, and your life that wills and legal documents cannot begin to approach.

Several studies have shown that using a financial planner adds value in areas such as designing a plan and having it followed, avoiding expensive mistakes, integrating financial information and presenting it in a way that allows clients to incorporate their beliefs and priorities into financial goals, thereby lowering their stress, and saving them money. The strategies that financial advisors use to help their clients achieve their goals include tax efficiency asset location, matching financial strategies to specific goals, and a cogent withdrawal strategy in retirement, etc. These improvements alone could improve a person's total welfare significantly. Where advisors really shine is by accurately assessing risk tolerance, making portfolio recommendations, helping their client focus on their goals, preventing their clients from inappropriate or knee-jerk reactions to market turmoil, retirement planning, estate planning, and recognizing insurance needs. Jim Kinney, a financial planner in New York emphasizes that a financial plan can help with almost every significant financial decision for an individual. A plan can relieve stress and anxiety, and reduces uncertainty while bringing clarity to financial decisions. An advisor also helps as a sounding board, a sort of devil's advocate. This helps clients understand the tradeoffs between their various financial and life goals. All of this adds to an improved quality of life allowing people to enjoy their life more fully. How do you quantify that?

I remember reading an article in the Wall Street Journal where the writer was interviewing a retiring very successful CEO. The writer asked the CEO if there was one thing he would do over, what it would be. The CEO responded that he would not miss his children's activities when they were growing up. Thirty years later, no one can remember what meeting took place when and what was discussed, but his kids remember that he did not show up to their soccer game or dance recital. Since then I have tried, and mostly succeeded, to live by that philosophy.

Chapter 18

What Is Right Works So Much Better Than What Is Wrong

৵ৡ৶

Contributor: Jeffrey Levy

*J*eff and I met a few years ago, and again quite recently. We share a passion for improving quality of life, and have had discussions on our different approaches. My background and training has been in quality improvement, where you identify a deficiency or something you want to make better, and then set goals for improvement. After reading Jeff's contribution to *If I Knew Then What I Know Now*, I better understand his philosophy and why he is so passionate about his work.

There is validity of the power of positive thinking, and finding the positive in our lives is so important. It is so true when Jeff talks about our society's focus on the negative. We do have a punitive system for anything we do wrong which is much stronger than the rewards system for what we do right.

The information Jeff shares in this chapter is able to be applied not only to our workplace, but to our home life, as well. In our business, it should be considered whether you are a staff person or a business owner. The "change has to start at the top" philosophy is out there, absolutely, but I think that our day would be much better no matter where the change starts; after all, many of us spend more hours at work than anywhere else. It is up to us whether we want to grumble about being at work and have a bad day because we hate the place, or if we want to be at work having a good day. Again, the same goes at home. Is it better to focus on what is "right" with our loved ones instead of always focusing on what is wrong?

I felt privileged to read Jeff's examples and clear ideas. What Jeff has shared about what he has learned in his life through his experience might just be what we need to make our lives happier!

— *Dawen*

Most of what we do in life is governed by our natural reactions – our "autopilot." A recent study at Duke University proclaimed that almost fifty percent of the things we do each day, we do automatically without conscious thinking.[13] We are creatures of autopilot.

The beauty of the human mind is that it enables us to do repetitive tasks without thinking, for example brushing our teeth, tying our shoes, or driving to work. How many times have you done something you do every day, but cannot remember doing it? We all have a tremendous innate ability to operate from a part of our brain that does not require conscious effort to think.

Here is where the stakes increase: our brains naturally detect things that bring us joy and things that cause us harm. This is the basic organizing principle of the brain – we subconsciously move toward pleasure and move away from threat. And, lucky for us, our brains are exceptionally good at sensing threats. When we are walking alone at night and hear a rustling in the bushes, we are immediately on guard and ready to either flee or fight. No thinking, no deciding, no planning – there is no time. It is either fight or flight.

Good things have no urgency: Good things, though, do not get such an immediate reaction. Unlike negative situations that cause our hearts to flutter, our breathing to quicken, and the hairs on the back of our neck to stiffen, good things often go unnoticed. Many of us are oblivious to good things because there is no urgency, no immediate need to react. Plus, our society teaches us not to be self-centered and not to brag. Whether we are paid a compliment, complete a tough project, or deliver a rousing speech, we are more inclined to be thankful for not screwing up than for doing a great job.

That is the problem: when we focus only on solving or fixing problems we limit our learning experiences to only negative events. Instead, we can learn so much more effectively and quicker by studying **what is right**.

Since any kind of danger automatically gets our immediate attention, we are, by default, a problem-focused society. Face it, problems get our attention. Managers proudly extol their great problem-solving skills, and school teachers assign students problems to solve. Give most people a compliment and they quickly offset it by admitting their perceived weaknesses. We need to learn how to learn from our **strengths**, because that is where our success comes from.

What I know now is that solving problems limits our ability to thrive and to flourish. The very best we can hope for when solving a problem is the absence of that problem, and nothing more.

At Her Wits End: Martin Seligman, the famous author, psychologist, and former president of the American Psychology Association and founder of Positive Psychology, said that just because you can cure someone of depression does not mean you can make them happy, they are two entirely different things.

My career is that of a management consultant, and I discovered the power of "what's right" thinking very early in my career, in the mid-1980s. I was on an assignment at a manufacturing company in a small town about 80 miles out of Atlanta. We were a team of four consultants, and our client was experiencing a big slump: lackluster sales, layoffs, and cut backs. Employee morale was at an all-time low. When we arrived and met with the president, his biggest fear was that we would give false hope to employees that, if they told us their concerns, the company would be able to fix all their problems. "They're going to tell you all of their problems," he lamented, "and I don't want them to think these problems will go away. I don't know if they'll ever go away," he confided.

After that emotional meeting with the president, we knew we had to avoid asking employees for their ideas and suggestions about what needs improvement. They would have volumes of ideas, but we would leave the company's management in a rough spot because they would not be able to act to do much.

Then the idea struck: Let us not look for what is wrong, let us find out what is right. The four of us interviewed employees for three consecutive days and asked them what was so good about this company? Why did they like working there? What was it was about the company that made it special? What would make it even more special?

We compiled all the answers we got and grouped them, and on the last day, we presented these findings to the president and his senior management team. While before we started, this management team thought our involvement would only make things worse, they now became speechless.

This group of senior executives could not believe the amount of passion, commitment, loyalty, and valuable ideas their employees had. "We never dreamed they cared so much," the president said. The information they now had gave them the tools to rebuild the company and involve the employees in the process. Employees suggested ways to improve quality, shorten cycle times, improve delivery times, and increase sales without spending any money. The executives, never in their wildest dreams, ever imagined a real solution being so close at hand.

This experience cut a deep trench within me and paved the way to transform the lives of many people since.

Another powerful story involved the owner of a day care center who transformed her business almost overnight. When we met her business was losing money, had an environment of poor morale, parent complaints, and a workplace no one looked forward to being at each day. The owner told me in no uncertain terms, "I'm at my wits end."

I gathered the owner, assistant director, and office manager in a small office where they complained that none of the employees took any kind of initiative. They complained, "If you don't tell them exactly what to do, they won't do anything." As I spoke with them, it became clear they habitually corrected people's mistakes and pointed out their faults. They were entirely problem focused.

So, here is how I avoided "fixing" the problem. I had them find their solution by looking at what is right, not what is wrong. I asked, "Tell me occasions when your staff takes initiative." The three women looked at each other in disbelief and reiterated, "They don't take initiative!"

I would not accept it. I asked again, "Come on, there must be something that they take initiative in doing?" And with that, the owner told me how the teachers take initiative to keep their classrooms clean. "Yes," the assistant director agreed, "They do a great job in keeping their classrooms clean."

Transformed the Business: Here is the secret: Figure out what it is that makes it work so well. I naturally asked, "Why do you think they do such a good job keeping their classrooms clean?" All three of them told me how the teachers received training when they first started to work there, how each received a check list of all the things they needed to keep organized, and how they have weekly inspections, and. . .

Within barely a few minutes, I saw light bulbs flash in their eyes. They stopped, looked at one another and began, "You know, we don't really communicate our expectations very much. . . and we haven't put that book of procedures together that we promised. . . and we don't ever tell them what a good job they're doing. . . and if we provided training on. . . ." Long story short: they figured out their problem without focusing on the problem.

They immediately began to reinforce the good things their employees did, and talk to them about how they did such a good job. In no time, people's passion and pride kicked in, and these improvements were reinforced by the three senior managers. For seven consecutive years since their "discovery", they have been operating in the black with excellent employee morale and very few, if any, parent complaints.

Do not be tempted to fixate on problems. What the mind dwells on only grows. Here is another case in point. I was asked to work with a museum where the executive director and her four-member management team did not get along – to the detriment of the museum. Fundraising was suffering, employee complaints were mounting, and public trust was at stake.

What Was the Best Part of Your Day? This particular group was so dysfunctional that two of the managers refused to talk with one another. Their only means of communication was to leave each other a voice mail or send an email. You can imagine the difficulties their employees had to endure. One of the first things that I did was to gather the five in a conference room and make a huge, gigantic list of everything they were proud of at the museum, and there was quite a lot they were proud of! They rallied together to make sure every bit of their excellent work appeared on the flip chart. This was the first major step, sharing and appreciating the good things they did.

What really brought them together was what I did next. I assigned each person the task of asking at least one employee each day for a full week, "What was the best part of your day?" I asked that they keep track of the responses they got, as well as the reactions, so we could talk about it the following week.

When I arrived the following week, they were all waiting in the conference room for me, but there was something distinctly different in their faces and in their demeanor. As I walked in, one of the two that did not speak with the other blurted out, "This has been the best week I've had since working here for the past six years!" For the next hour, they shared stories about the impact this question had made, not only on the people they asked, but on them too. One told me how an employee started to cry because she had such a touching and endearing experience that day helping a woman in a wheel chair. Another told me how the employee thanked her for asking that question because it had meant so much to her.

Without focusing on the problems that divided this management team, they magically came together, and on their own, broke down whatever walls that had kept them apart. They went on to work together to increase fundraising for the museum and to implement a new exhibit that was quite the talk of the town.

Here is the Point: So, here is the point: Do not get suckered into the problem-fixing trap; instead, whatever the problem, look for incidents and examples where the problem did not exist. If you want to fix a quality problem, investigate when quality was at its best. Why was it so good? What was going on? What was different than the way it is now? If someone is always late to work, examine what was happening when they arrived on time. If a student is not doing well in a class, examine what was going on in a class in which they performed well.

Here is the formula:

1) What is right?
2) What makes it right?
3) What would be ideal?

Pay attention and study the reasons and situations where things work well. Ask, "What did we do to make it work so well?" Do not waste time figuring out what was done to break it, or why "Sally" is always late to work, or why quality is a problem with a particular product. When you know what it takes to make it right, the reason for it not being right does not matter.

When we focus on what is right, our brains release chemicals that make us think faster, more broadly, more creatively, and more optimistically. When we focus on problems, our energy becomes depleted. Our shoulders slump, our enthusiasm drains. But when we focus on what is right, and what makes it right, we become energized.

Begin today with trying this simple exercise. Just ask someone, "What was the best part of your day?"

Chapter 19

What Do You Want To Be When You Grow Up?

Contributor: Brian Cohen

*T*here are people who know what they want to be when they grow up from the time they are very young, like my husband, Jim. He knew he wanted to be a police officer by the time he was nine years old. His mother has told me many stories of how he would purposely get lost in department stores so he could find the security guards so he could hang out with them. That was certainly not me. I personally spent most of my life trying to figure out what I wanted to be when I grew up.

Remember when you were little and someone would come up to you and say, little girl / boy, what do you want to be when you grow up? What did you answer – an astronaut, a ballerina, a firefighter? Always so much pressure, even then. How did you know what to choose? In Brian's story, this is the question he poses to the reader.

Recently I was privileged to hear the New York State Education Commissioner speak. A question that is being asked today is what our students need from our schools to succeed in business and higher education. It appears that we need to do more to make our students career ready and to provide them with skills and pathways to success. This is not new. I remember graduating from high school and feeling like, "voilà", you are now on your own. Remember how it felt, if you had the opportunity to go to college, looking through the course catalog, trying to choose a career? My son Gregory experienced this. He has changed his major in college three times, extending his four year undergraduate degree to a projected six year time period. Although he is not graduating on schedule, I consider him very lucky to find his career path so early in life.

This is not so easy for others, as we will see in Brian's account of his struggle to find his passion for his career. I met Brian by accident at a Toastmasters meeting. Ever since I joke with him about his ability to help others speak in public. If you do some research, you will find that people fear public speaking more than death. Really, there are actual articles about this — I am not kidding. Without disclosing too much of Brian's story, you will learn that public speaking is a most important activity in his life. If we look deep enough, we all have a passion and a gift within us. I consider those of us who can take that gift or passion and create a livelihood surrounding it brave and the luckiest of all. So many people take a job or get "stuck" in a career they do not enjoy just so they can earn a salary.

Brian's account of his search for a career that will bring him happiness is not only heartfelt, but I know what he has identified and what he knows now will help so many.

— Doreen

If I knew then what I know now? This question would be a mute point, and so would the question of my career path. Maybe, just maybe, if I paid attention throughout my life, things would have wound up different. Perhaps you can ask yourself the same question I should have asked myself a long time ago: Do you take time to consider what brings you joy and not just a paycheck?

It is interesting that, when I look back, I can see so many examples over the years of what I am lucky to now enjoy doing. I have been thinking of this and wonder if my enjoyment today was different, would my recollection of past events also be different? Certainly, I am doing a lot of wondering right now, and I would much prefer to answer the question with concrete, actionable ideas.

If I knew then what I know now, first and foremost, I would have kept a journal. Flat out, that would have been the smartest thing I could have ever done. The amount of time it would have taken on a daily basis would have been minimal, but the knowledge I would have gained would have been immeasurable.

I do hope and expect that got your attention. If not, then ask yourself this: Can you recall all of the little things that happened to you last year, five years ago or even longer than that? Do you remember the things that have had an impact on you? My guess is that there are certain highlights that you do recall, certainly the positive ones, but what about the negatives? Do you recall them as quickly? Probably not, yet they are just as important as the positive ones. Our negative occurrences are also are a part of the fabric that makes us who we are today.

My best negative was being promoted to the position of Sales Manager. It truly was one of the most exciting promotions that I ever received up to that point in my life. It validated a great deal of the work that I was doing in the office where I worked, but also brought out a rather significant shortcoming. I was a boring speaker. Luckily I became aware of this very specific and important area where I certainly needed improvement and did something about it. As of the time of this writing, I have gone from a boring speaker to host various radio and television shows. I have even successfully performed on a comedy stage!

My newly found skills and self-improvement all came about because I identified a need. Yet, still, the question remained. How did I wind up in a situation where I was giving sales presentations? If I had paid attention to my life situations while they were happening, would I have been more prepared for the opportunity or would I have gone down a different career path?

Since we are in the here and now, it would be impossible to start over again, and since I did not keep a diary from childhood, I did the next best thing. I broke out my old photo albums. I am sure I am dating myself. I am in my fifties and used to take pictures with film, have it processed and then put the photos into a photo album. Archaic, yes, but this exercise was able to spark important memories. Another trip down memory lane was through my school yearbooks, paying particular attention to the comments friends made. If you think this suggestion is something you want to try, also take into consideration the clubs, organizations, committees, sports or any after school activities you joined. Invariably, while looking at this material, you might find yourself making comments like, I really enjoyed that, hated this, and asked yourself what you were doing there. Smile! It is all good. This walk down memory lane gave me, and hopefully will give you, a little insight into what brought joy then, and hopefully what still does, or could, bring you joy today.

In my case, I found pictures and situations where I was on stage or "leading the way". I played Christopher Columbus in fourth grade, an ad-libbed role, and I enjoy performing "improv" comedy today. I also sang in chorus in seventh grade, not well, but still remember enjoying my time on stage. In college, I was master of ceremonies (MC) for a talent show and a variety of dorm events. You would think, from this, I would have realized that I enjoyed the limelight. You would be right, but I did not know then what I know now.

The examples like that are many, but it took me 25 years and a promotion to a position that I was not good at to get me to take action. Was it a "waste" of 25 years, or was I learning other things along the way that continue to make me who I am today?

If someone asked me what I want to be when I grow up. My friend Tom Fabbri wrote a book called *The Ageless You*, which assumes that we are ageless. If so, maybe I do not have to worry about being too old to change my career focus.

We all have met with them through the years: guidance counselors, career placement advisors, and our moms and dads. I can recall meeting the guidance counselors in junior high school, but if, memory serves correct, it was about grades and nothing about a desire that would guide my career path. I think it would have been helpful if we focused on <u>why</u> I found it easier to study for some subjects rather than others. This realization became clearer when I looked back now at how I did in college. I realize I accomplished what "I had to do" in some classes, and that I really enjoyed others. As a rule of thumb, I realize now that I had enjoyed the classes that were more interactive. I never "took" to the lecture style classes, regardless of the topic, but I loved making class presentations, which I did on many occasions, and I remember them all.

Are you getting guidance from your team? In hindsight I wish I interacted more during that period in my life. So the magical question is, who should you speak to and why? In my experience I found my parents sometimes very challenging to speak with. Part of their guidance may be based on wanting you to succeed in things that they wanted to do but did not. They want may you to succeed and try new ventures, but only if you will not fail. I will expand on that later, but if you are in such a cloistered environment where failing is not an option, then it will be very hard for you to achieve a major success. Yet, on the other hand, if you have a relationship with your parents that allows for an open and honest conversation about risk and why it should be embraced, not feared, then talk. In that situation they may be your best resource, as they may know you better than anyone else, at least in your earlier years.

What about your friends? At sixteen anything seems possible, at twenty one we are still finding ourselves, at twenty five, who knows? At this stage I would say no to asking friends for guidance. Look at it this way. If you make the assumption that your friends know what they want, you may be encouraged to go along with them for their ride. Is that really going to help you achieve your desires? The only way I will say yes to that statement is if you know what and who you are. For me, I was still looking, and sadly I was listening to others much more than I was listening to myself. My standard answer was that I did not know what I wanted out of life, and the reality is that I did not. This state puts us into a very vulnerable position. If one of my friends came along with a strong idea I would have followed along, probably more for their sake and not mine. Take your time with friends at this stage. Some twenty year olds are so set on their dream that success is inevitable. That is terrific. If you are one of them, then you are blessed. Most will need to find their own way. Take into account what people are saying, not what just one person is telling you.

We have discussed family, friends and counselors, but let me give you one idea that is slightly different. Go to job fairs, industry events and trade shows. I had no idea what was out there when I was in my twenties, but what if I had attended business shows? What would I have found? What can you find? Attend them with the attitude that you are not there to find a job, but that a career path will find you. Forget money, forget experience, and disregard any other obstacle. Attending business events such as these may just open your eyes to a world you never knew existed.

I was once asked if I needed additional training on a new computer system installed at my office. I could not answer that question. How did I know what I did not know? We were never given the opportunity to review the programs beforehand. I did not know what the programs even were, so how could I ask for training? Same holds true for careers, if you do not know what is out there, how can you find it? How would you know what you like if you do not try it? Brussel sprouts come to mind here.

How can you know what you will excel at or what you enjoy if you do not give yourself a chance to learn?

I wish someone told me to pay attention to what I really learned on each venture. At this point, the word "failure" comes into mind. If I knew then what I know now, I would understand that the best lessons come from a less than desired outcome.

I do not aim for failure, but one must understand that not everything we do is going be a success. At least, perhaps not in the way we expect it to be. Learn from life, learn from your mistakes, learn from everything you do.

In high school I was afraid of failure, so I focused on being liked. There could have been worse things to be, but what if someone told me to take a chance, what is the worst that can happen? *__Really__*, what is the worst that can happen? We are not talking about flying a plane here or climbing a mountain. We are just talking about trying to achieve more than what you **THINK** you are capable of. Why do we short-change ourselves? Is it because we are afraid of failure? Do we think, "Don't be afraid, but don't ever fail?"

True failure does not come in not achieving your goal; it comes from not learning from what keeps you from it. This ties into where we started, keeping a diary. There are three ways that we learn from our projects:

Learn by achieving: That is obvious and fruitful. Mom always told me this one. If you are good at something and enjoy it, keep going. It is an easy way to grow.

Learn by a less than desired outcome: I do not recall anyone telling me this as often as I needed to hear it. Identify where there had been a shortcoming, and focus on that to learn what you need to do differently.

And. . . this is it — the big one that I really did wish I knew then but know now.

Identify what part of the project you enjoyed doing the most and were the most proficient in: This may be the direction to which your whole life should be headed.

Let us go way back to when I played Christopher Columbus. Remember that was in fourth grade. What I did not do terribly well was act. What I recall the most was making eye contact, and that I was most interested in having everyone follow me. What I wish I knew then that I know now is that I can connect with an audience, but it took me almost forty years after my role as Columbus to learn that. Thankfully I do not believe that I learned too late. I have found my true passion, a path for a career that I now pursue, a new focus.

What I know now that I wish I knew then was that we must learn from everything that we do. It could be a raging success, but if we are not excited by it, then that is not "it". I have learned that something could be a complete failure, and that why it failed may be our learning experience. I have learned that, sometimes, what we unexpectedly learn brings us the biggest gift of them all - our true calling.

I know now that life is, and always will be, a learning experience. Take whatever steps you need to remember your past and current situations. Use a diary, a living business plan or pictures to learn from. Also, be open to taking on new challenges. My role as a sales manager changed my life, but it was not the sales manager role that did it. It was what I learned from being boring speaker.

I now know that anything is possible. I hope your "when" is now to find your passion and hope your learning curve is shorter than mine.

Section 4

Conclusion

৵ৡ৵

"I am a Victor, Not a Victim" ~ Joel Osteen

Chapter 20

Digging Deeper

❧

*D*igging deeper, it is only recently that I have had the ability to identify the underlying reasons why I have been "striving for the brass ring". I had said we were going back to: **Children Learn What They Live,** and this is a recount of some of my experiences growing up, what I learned through them, and the evolution of how they made me into a "people-pleaser" instead of a Doreen pleaser. I do not remember much of my childhood, and although there surely were plenty of positive occurrences, these highlights are most vivid in my recollection. It has taken me a long time to realize how I started living my life proving instead of pleasing myself and to stop enabling others to make me feel inferior. Perhaps you will see yourself in some of my reflections, perhaps it will spark an "aha!" moment in you to realize why you may be doing something in your life and inspire your transformation. I believe this was my journey from being a tortured soul to becoming free.

My siblings and I grew up in a household where "children are seen and not heard". If we went visiting, even if you were dying of thirst, you would say, "No thank you," if you were asked if you wanted anything. We did have manners, please and thank you, but this was manners on steroids. I realize my conditioning when I was younger by not asking for anything carried forward throughout my life. I believe it was a primary reason for my not being powerful or "allowed" to ask for what I have wanted or needed. In some ways this is still a battle for me to this day. I realize now that, as my children were growing up, I have unconsciously made them ask for things. When we went somewhere I always had them go up to a representative and ask for what they needed. When we went out to dinner I always had them order their own meals. I'll never forget how proud I was the first time my son Nicholas was able to ask for extra honey-mustard for his chicken nuggets. They are not bashful about asking for what they need. They are strong. I realize now that there is power behind asking for what we want. The alternative is living with hard feelings when we do not.

I started babysitting when I was 11 years old, as I was one of the oldest kids living in our new development on Long Island. Once I had money I started chipping in to buy my own clothing. My parents, at that time, did support me, and we had a lovely home in a nice suburban area. I worked during the summers and, again, enjoyed having money and freedom. My dad was not around much as he was always "working". Unfortunately, in my later years, I realized he was out dating other women. My father's cheating left a huge impression on me. One thing I told Jim before we were married was that if he ever wanted to go out with someone else, not to cheat on me, but to tell me. It is better to let someone go than to live with disrespect, and it is my opinion that cheating is complete and utter disrespect. I am sure there are many reasons why people cheat, not only in relationships, but in all aspects of life. Try as a person might, there is no justification to validate cheating. There are many articles and books written about cheating, and I am not going to go into this in detail, as it is just too big of a subject. People have to recognize cheating as a selfish behavior that hurts all the people involved, no matter what the circumstances, business or personal. Enough said.

I know things were not the best between my parents. I appreciate that my father stayed as long as he did. However, there is a right way to leave a relationship and a wrong way. My dad chose the wrong way.

My mom did the best she could without herself ever having much of a childhood. She had grown up too fast, becoming pregnant with me when she was only seventeen. As I look back and reflect on conversations we had shared, I now realize that she has always been a tortured soul living under the shadow of her brother being the favorite child. Her parents have been gone a long time, and I know she has never been able to escape the feeling of not being important to them. Whether it was real or fabricated, it was real to her. It is not easy for kids or people to not feel important. To this day, I believe she justifies her importance by having "things", a house, a car, jewelry. Material things do not satisfy the emptiness in a person's heart. There are many books on this, too. If you recognize yourself in this situation you might consider seeing a counselor or reading some books on the subject. It is important to change your beliefs about yourself to start to be able to change your life.

As a result I grew up learning envy instead of appreciation of what others accumulated because of their hard work, achievements or sacrifice. As I got older, I was lucky enough to learn, and fully believe that we should support the achievements of others, not envy them, but to work together to make our lives better. I now live with a vision of "people helping people" where we work together to support each other in our missions and dreams. I learned that envy is poison to our well being. It stops us from our own momentum and success. This is not a generalization or a blanket statement. There is so much evidence out there regarding how entire communities are beaten down because "these people "or "those people" do not believe they can change things. There is power when people work together, more power than one person can achieve independently. I believe it is up to us, together, to make things change and not wait for someone else to do it for us. It has been said that waiting gets us nowhere.

I know times were different when I was a child. I loved my grandparents very much, but they yelled at each other unmercifully. My mom learned what she knew, and yelling was commonplace when we did not do what she wanted. I constantly walked on eggshells, never knowing when I would do something wrong, or when I would be considered "bad". Early on with my kids I found myself to be a yeller. Thankfully, for me, I stopped that at some point in their youth. I do not yell anymore. I broke the cycle, and I believe they will not yell either. I have learned it is not healthy for the yeller and it is not productive way to motivate others or get them to listen to you, at home or at work. Many of us are or were yellers. We may do as we learn, and it is up to us to determine if what we are doing works for us in our lives or if we need to adopt a different approach.

As a child, I also learned fear of failure and that I always had to be BETTER, that I always had to shine to get attention or recognition from my father. When I was young I struggled in math and in the tenth grade earned a "D" in geometry. I was punished for an entire semester until my next report card came. The math grade was just one example of punishment where I had things taken away, and through these experiences I learned that I could never fail. I do not believe a punishment like that was a very progressive way to help a child grow or succeed. Instead, help and support would have been a better way for my parents to have dealt with my struggles. Jeff Levy covered a positive approach to change in his chapter, *What's Right Works So Much Better Than What's Wrong*. I realize now that if a particular approach hasn't worked for us in situations in the past, it may be time to try something different.

I know that my husband and I have tried to prepare our children to go into the world the best we could. With strict rules in my home as a child, I felt unprepared for experiences I faced. For example, not dating until I was sixteen left me scared, not confident, and even a bit embarrassed to speak to boys. I am not saying that children should not have rules, we all need boundaries. However, I truly believe that people, no matter their age, need to be able to consider their options to be able to make the best choices for themselves and what may happen when we make a bad choice, as well. I realize that no matter how much a parent tries to shelter or protect a child in their early years, there will be situations where they will need to make the right choices for their own safety or well being. They need to be emotionally equipped with tools and knowledge they can reference. I worked with a wise man who frequently said, "If you don't have the tools you can't do the job." I believe this is something that can be applied across the board both physically and emotionally. It is a founding principal of Time to Play. Learn what you need to know so you can enjoy life. I believe it is our responsibility to teach those in our care and, if appropriate, those in our path, so they can become successful in whatever situation they may face.

Remember that there is always a root cause for everything. I have spent a lot of effort breaking down what I experienced that caused me to have obstacles in my life. It has taken me a long time to feel comfortable talking to people or to stand up for myself. I am grateful that I was able to recognize and change my undesirable behavior. I am proud that I now have the power to choose whether to address something and move forward to take action in a situation, or to not address it at all.

I will never forget the day my father left us for good. These are the highlights of things emblazoned in my mind that occurred over a period of time and led up to that day. I know now that there is a right way and a wrong way to end a relationship or deal with a problem. Looking back now we should have realized and addressed things that were happening. I know now that you cannot ignore situations that are happening in your life. Problems do not just go away but fester and become harder to deal with when they finally "hit the fan".

My mom did not deal with anger well. Again, I think it was based on what she learned in her childhood with my grandparents yelling at each other. As I noted, my mother always yelled, and there were frequent arguments between her and my father. These experiences were not emotionally healthy for me or my three siblings. I am the oldest, my sisters are four years and seven years younger than me, and my brother is thirteen years younger. You may have read his chapter, *Lost . . . then Found*. Sometimes we are so close to a situation and cannot see the big picture. In personal or business relationships it may be important to look around and see how our individual behavior is affecting others. I believe we instinctively know when we can make things better.

As I previously noted, I know my father cheated on my mother for many years. I used to be so proud to go to work with my father and "help" at his mechanic shop. As we have read many times throughout this book, many of us idolized our fathers. My father was my idol when I was younger, as well. A few times when I went to work with him he had a woman (I think it was the same one) take me out for the day for haircuts or shopping. We even went to a barbecue with her family once, and when I was thirteen he brought me to see the movie *Grease* on a date with her. Being thirteen, I did not realize anything was wrong, but I do recall experiencing very uncomfortable feelings. While I am sure my father had the best of intentions in taking me along, in retrospect, those experiences affected me significantly. While raising my children I have been careful to live by example and I realize that, perhaps, these experiences are why I have refrained from participating in some activities or became known as a "goody two shoes". I know now how important it is for us to realize how simple things can deeply affect a child or another person and how we need to be aware of what experiences we impose on others.

I also realized how I could trace feelings of self doubt about my own importance back to the day my father made me late for my high school graduation. He arrived home late from work and we had to rush to get there. We lived only three miles away from the school. The day was so hot, and we had to go up the stairs to the football field. My aunt put hair pins in to hold my hat in place – there is a picture of this occurrence, freezing it in time, in my school's yearbook supplement. I was supposed to be most important that day, but the event turned from being joyous to inconvenient and disappointing. I remember sweating the entire ceremony, and, to this day, cannot think about it without wondering if he made me late because he was out with a girlfriend.

I also now realize that my not being allowed to go away to college like many of my high school friends may be why I wholeheartedly encourage others to pursue their talents or their dreams. Not only do I believe my overprotective mom did not trust me to go away, but she verbalized how my brother was going to have to support a family one day and how he needed to go away to school. That was the 1960s thinking, not 1980s thinking. In the '80s and today, women are not just caretakers, and many women at that time and in our society today do not have the opportunity to be stay-at-home moms. I did a "woe is me" for many years blaming everyone else because I did not feel I had become whatever I thought I should have, not being proud of myself, and not seeing the great things I actually achieved. **But here is the key – after so many years I finally realized it.** Just because someone tells you that you cannot or should not do or be something, it really is up to you to bring your potential to reality. **<u>Who made me not pursue something? ME. I did it. I let it happen</u>**. Remember I now believe that in most cases where there is a will, there is a way.

As I grew older I started to realize things a little more. I was still living at home, but my father was not. He would come home on the weekends, as "it was too hard for him to travel". He had set up his mechanic's shop about a forty minute drive from our home where "the rich people lived". We used to live pretty well at that time, with him bringing home a decent salary. In 1983 when I was sixteen years old we were sitting around the kitchen table. He told a story about how the "tax man" was going to come to get us because he had not paid the taxes for the business and how my mother should take a second mortgage so there was no equity in the house. I still feel responsible, as a sixteen year old, butting into the conversation, being scared of the "tax man", and trusting my father. I remember my father telling us how he would set up a bank account to keep the money in it, $40,000, which should come out of the equity of the house that would pay back the loan. I remember commenting that it was probably a good idea, after all, the "tax man" sounded really scary. My mom went along with it. Maybe I had something to do with the decision for her to proceed, which to this day, hurts my soul. Who would have expected he would lie to us? After all, aren't parents supposed to take care of their family?

You would think this experience would make me fearful of trusting others, but I realize it has actually had the reverse affect on me. I realize that, throughout my life, I have so desperately wanted to trust others that time and time again I wind up with hurt feelings or making bad business decisions. I guess my behavior could have gone either way. This realization can be broadened to actions, laws or decisions we implement individually or as a society. Everything is based on evidence or drawing on past experiences. Perhaps we need to consider the true root of our actions. Even as I am writing this, I know I will be able to apply even more awareness to my actions moving forward.

My story's not over. There is more. It gets worse. Early on in the first semester of my enrollment at our community college, without really knowing the circumstances surrounding my actions, I remember calling my father one evening from a pay phone at the college. I remember asking him if he was going to leave us and leave me with this family. I remember his words, "No, sweetie, I would never do that." My mother did not work. She had no college education. My sisters at the time were thirteen, ten, and my brother was four. I can actually still see and feel myself in the phone booth during the conversation like it happened yesterday.

A few days later, my mother got a call from my grandfather. My mother's parents lived in Florida, and my grandma had been a heavy smoker and she had been sick for a while. She had a heart attack and valve surgery, and was fighting cancer. One morning my mom got a call that she had died. My grandma was one of my favorite people, and I was always important to her. I still can feel her embrace and her kisses. She used to smother me in them. Now she was gone. My mom called my father, who was not living at home. She asked him to come home, that her mother had died. At that very moment he said no and told her he was leaving her. He not only left her, he left all of us, only a few days from that phone call I made from my college. He lied to me but, no matter how bad a relationship may be, it is inconceivable that he could have left my mother the day her mother died. Remember how I said there is a right way and a wrong way to leave a relationship? This was really the wrong way, and the way it played out is a vision forever etched in my mind.

I have to note that my father's dad left his mother when he was thirteen years old. History repeats itself **if we let it**. There are better ways to do things. His actions, no matter how he could have justified them to himself, were 1,000% wrong. And, the way he left after all those years of marriage, after years of cheating, lying, and more, was unforgivable. That is how I started hating him. I hated him since he had left in 1983, and he did not even know. He did not even care. Hating him hurt no one but me.

My mom, sisters and brother flew to Florida for my grandmother's funeral. I stayed at home to make sure he did not come home and clean out our house, as at that point we did not know what he would do. Thankfully, I had Jim who was my boyfriend at that time. Why he stayed with me through all this I still cannot figure out. We had only been dating for a few months, and here I was, seventeen years old with so much to deal with. I know Jim was Heaven sent. He has cared for me and guided me through my life, always protecting me. We have grown up together, to a certain extent. We are best friends, and I am very privileged to have him in my life.

Things were hard for quite a while. Remember how this book started? Who makes life hard? YOU DO! I know I did. I quit college so I could get a full time job to pay for the first of the two mortgages on my mother's house. I never had to drop out, but I did. In my mind, it was the best thing I could do at that time. In retrospect, it had been the wrong choice. I wish there had been a book like this that showed another person going through a similar situation. I wish I could have thought to look for a resource to tap into for guidance, a place that could have sparked me to identify that I needed to snap out of my "pity party". I wish someone would have pointed out that, yes, I was in a situation, but that I had the power to change it. My family and those surrounding me at the time were all consumed by our new life situation that we just went through the motions of daily survival. I wish someone had been there to offer some additional guidance. I wish someone from the outside offered "food for thought" to help me deal with all I had to at the time in my life; hence this book and my development of Time to Play, a place to find resources for a better life so we can enjoy our life. As it relates to college, looking back now I realize I could have taken even one class at a time. I did not have to quit entirely. I did not go back to complete my associate's degree for eight years, and it took me a total of twenty years before I finally earned my master's degree.

I made that choice. It did not have to be that way. I let my power be taken. When I finished my degrees it was more to prove to my father that I did it, that I made it, and that I did not fail in my life, to show that I was good enough. I had to PROVE it, the recurring theme of my life, proving instead of living. I had to make myself feel important, achievement after achievement that I could tout, always in the back of my mind believing that I was not worthy.

My grandfather chipped in to pay for the second mortgage. My mom started cleaning houses. We had food stamps and we got scarves from the PTA. We did not know if my father was alive for quite a while or even where he was. We had no money but continued to pay his life insurance just in case he did something rash. As far as we were concerned he must have been depressed, or something else, to leave his whole family. Horrible to think about, but justified in our minds. Here we thought he was suicidal for leaving us, but he was not. He was living the good life. He took the $40,000 from the second mortgage out of the bank. We later found out he bought a boat and that he and his girlfriend moved to Texas. At that time Texas had the most lenient child support laws and we learned he had apparently performed a lot of research and preparation prior to leaving us. He just did not make any provisions to make sure his family was taken care of before he left. He just abandoned us, and it had not mattered to him if we starved or became homeless.

The frustration of our new financial situation was unrelenting. When my mom would pay the second mortgage, my father would draw out of it. My mother was finally, somehow, able to get his name off the account so he could not keep taking out funds. I really do not know how she made it through, and how she found a way for us to keep our house, for which I am eternally grateful.

Eventually, she met a nice gentleman and remarried. My parents had not been officially divorced at the point when my mother wanted to marry my stepfather. She could not afford to pay for the divorce, and my father said he would not pay for it. My mom and her future husband scraped together money to pay for the divorce. As I recall, my mom and step-father later learned that my father married the woman he had moved to Texas with *the day before* their wedding.

Even with the ups and downs in their relationship, my mom and her husband have been together over twenty-five years. Once they were remarried, I moved out. I was approaching my nineteenth birthday. I lived in a little studio apartment around the corner from Jim and his family. My now mother and father-in-law watched out for me. I am grateful that all worked out well and that Jim and I stayed together, even under the circumstances.

I continued through my life, getting married, going back to pursue my education and having our children. I moved up in my career, but waited for people to recognize my talents to promote me. It has been a hard learning experience. As previously discussed, I learned that people will not just hand you things. Don't be bashful. You have to ask for what you need, set goals, and pursue what you want out of life. It is up to you.

"Life Is What You Make of It" ~ Unknown

I have learned that I could not control the events of my childhood, but I could have controlled what I chose to do and how I reacted to everything. I realize now that I did not put a plan together, and just went into survival mode. I realize today you need a plan to survive, with goals and a vision you want to achieve. Nothing should stop a person from accomplishing, achieving, or doing whatever they want in life. Nothing should stop you. Go back to the "where there is a will there is a way" statement. Nothing should stop you – the only thing that stops us is ourselves.

"We are our own worst enemy" ~ Louis Binstock

I know I have been my own worst enemy, robbing myself of joy and happiness, subconsciously letting underlying beliefs run my life. It did not matter how good my life was, these negative beliefs were there, haunting me. I have said it a number of times, that I am happy I finally realized this and woke up before it was too late.

My sisters had their own individual experiences, and both moved out of mom's house young in order to escape a negative living situation. I am not going to go into their experiences. To this day I know, although she tries, my mother still battles her demons, and I am thankful that my brother managed to save himself.

It took me almost thirty years to realize that I had such deep rooted hatred for my father. I blamed him for everything and anything that did not go my way. Of course, nothing in my life was _my_ fault, right? I guess, deep down, I felt tremendous rejection. I read about forgiving and how forgiving frees your soul, but could not let it go.

I am sharing the following with the hopes that you will try the exercise to free yourself. Let us start with this quote:

Life is short, break the rules, forgive quickly, kiss slowly, love truly, laugh uncontrollably, and never regret anything that made you smile. Twenty years from now you will be more disappointed by the things you did not do than by the ones you did. So throw off the bowlines. Sail away from the safe harbor. Catch the trade winds in your sails. Explore. Dream. Discover.

~ Mark Twain

There is so much truth in this, and I hope you take it to heart.

Since I started my "quest for quality of life" I have attended many seminars and have read many books. Maybe I was finally open to change and ready to snap out of the blame game. I attended a seminar where there had been an exercise where we were asked to write about a great emotional issue that concerned money. Of course I wrote about how my father stole the $40,000 from us, that we almost lost our home, and how I had to pay the mortgage. I learned that my fear of not having money developed during this early time in my life. I know now that this fear had kept me from taking chances in business and in my career choices; I played it safe. This further demonstrates how there may be an underlying root cause that drives our decisions in everything we do or do not do throughout our life.

We were then asked to write a letter to the person who hurt us as if they wrote it to us themselves. I wrote the following on behalf of my father, as if he wrote it to me:

> *"I hated my life situation, and after years of taking care of everyone else felt I needed to get out. So, maybe I did it the wrong way, but I, at the time, did not really think I had another choice. I regret not seeing my family grow and being so segregated when I should have been a father."*

I know it does not sound like much. I did not detail the long sordid story or the negative living situation he experienced before he left us. I also could have put in how proud he was of me, as I know now that lacking that reassurance negatively impacted me in my life, but I did not even have to go into it.

After we wrote it, we had to read it to someone, and I read my short, not detailed statement to Jim. These three simple sentences were enough to finally free me. It was done. I recommend that you try and write a letter to yourself from someone who cannot, or may not, be able to communicate with you. Put in what you need to hear. You will be surprised at the results.

By my choice, my father and I had not spoken in many years. A few days after the seminar I called him to read him what he "wrote" to me. He apologized. At the end of our conversation I told him I closed the book on hating him. I no longer hated him. I no longer hurt. I no longer trapped myself in the past.

Am I perfect? Not at all, but are any of us perfect? Like I have said a few times, I am grateful enough to now know when I need to change or address something that is bothering me even though it might take a day or two to realize it. Wasting so much time feeling bad is just not an option for me anymore, and it should not be for you, either.

I know I went through what I did for a reason. I believe it was so I could help people recognize when they have lost their power so they can recover it. My only regrets are that it took me so long to get over the negative feelings I harbored and that I allowed myself to be a victim for way too long. I now know I could have moved on many years ago.

All in all, I am truly appreciative of how things turned out. If things were different, if I did go away to college, if he did not leave, I would not have the wonderful life I have now.

I think that is another way we have to look at things. We are on a journey. Sometimes it works out as we plan; sometimes it works out as God plans for us.

Things Happen for a Reason: This is not a cop out. Things do happen for a reason. But we do need to look at the "things" that happen. It is our choice if we are going to let them paralyze us, or let them be stepping stones to improve our lives. It is our choice to let things haunt us for thirty years, like I did, or to let things go. It is our choice to live in a situation that is displeasing, or to change things to make our lives better.

That is the Time to Play philosophy. Learn what you need to know so you can enjoy life. There is no time like the present. It is time to Enjoy YOUR Life.

Parting Words

If I Knew Then What I Know Now: I now know that a mind is a terrible thing to waste, but it may sometimes be a terrible thing to have. I have learned that our thoughts can keep us from rising to our full potential; that we can create our own prisons, sentencing us to live as tortured souls.

This realization has amazed me. I never realized it was **me**, *only me*, holding **me** back. If you have not gotten anything else from this book, I hope that you have started to understand this concept. I hope you can begin to find ways to start quieting the thoughts that hold **you** back and hold **you** down. I hope you realize your power within, perhaps untapped, to pursue your dreams and to make your mark. You know, it is never too late. I recently researched the oldest person who finished college. It was a ninety-nine year old man. He did it. He accomplished a dream. Do not disqualify the dream that is in your heart.

"If you dream it, you can do it." ~ Walt Disney

And, also just as important, help another along, too. If we each re-empower another person along the way, we will all be able to enjoy life. You know who needs it. You know the person who always seems overwhelmed or "down in the dumps". Talk to them. Maybe they just need someone to talk to or a little strength, encouragement or reassurance. We do not know what they have gone through in their day or in their life situation. Maybe it was not even a big deal, but we know now that our minds can make a mountain out of a molehill.

Our power is meant to share with others. Like the stories in this book, what we have learned and what we have shared might start you on a new path. Your story, or your kind word, might help another start on their new path, too. After all, we are all in this together.

There is one last idea I would like to leave you with. Have you ever heard the common phrase *"pay yourself first"*? Since we are a society that revolves around money, I thought this phrase was a great trigger to remind us to enjoy life and not do the things that do not make us happy. What does that mean? It is something easy to remember that will remind you when you need to make a change.

When I first heard "pay yourself first", I only understood it to mean monetarily. I have started using it in everything throughout my day as a "check". I recommend that you "Pay" yourself first" – spiritually, in happiness, in love, in satisfaction, in what you choose as your job, and in general in your life.

Do you like doing something? Whatever it is, if it makes you happy you are paying yourself. If it does not, you are losing "funds".

"Pay" yourself by exercising.

"Pay" yourself by eating healthy.

These things are only expensive when they are unpaid. We pay for everything else. Perhaps it is time you pay yourself. . . first.

I am so thankful and I will be eternally grateful that we were able to finally complete and share this book. It has been a gift for all of us to write it.

Like the cover of this book which is symbolic of our journey, I pray that we can all find the power to scale our mountains and eliminate anything standing in our way from reaching victory at the summit.

With much love and happiness,

— Dawn

P.S.: Need more? We are here for you!
Visit www.TimetoPlay.com for resources for a better life.

"Where there is a dream, there is an opportunity"
~ Doreen Guma

Contributor Biographies

Most of the contributors for this book also are professional resources on www.timetoplay.com

*J*onathan Barrett: Currently studying for a Master's in Theological Studies (Pastoral) at Liberty University in Lynchburg, Virginia (class of 2014). Jonathan served as a fill-in Preacher at Neriah Baptist Church in Buena Vista, VA in 2012. He is a graduate of the University of Alabama with a Bachelor of Science in Communications and he lives in Lynchburg, Virginia with his wife Sarah and two daughters, Katelyn and Rebecca. Jonathan is Doreen's brother.

Geena Bean: Geena is a children's book author, publishing *Come Back Dear Sun*. She is a graduate from Rutgers University and has been working with children for over ten years as a nanny. She enjoys helping kids make their stories become real through the use of their imagination. When she is not too busy fighting off pirates on old, rusty ships, or escaping from the doom of a deserted island where those wicked pirates have hidden her away, she is saving the world, one imagination at a time! Geena publicly speaks regarding the need for children to enjoy play time, not just computer time. She also has been performing book readings at elementary schools.

Madeline Brady: Madeline lives with her husband, Ralph, of forty-seven years in Mt. Sinai, New York. They have three married children and six grandsons. Madeline has a background in several areas of both the private and non-for-profit healthcare industry with more than twenty-five years experience in the healthcare field. Madeline and her husband have lived on LI for over forty years and enjoy leisure and travel. They have toured China and countries throughout Europe, the Caribbean and many U.S. States. Madeline enjoys being active in kickboxing and cardio workouts at her gym. Madeline and Ralph have instilled a love for education and physical activity in their family. All three children and their spouses are involved in running, yoga and physical training. Madeline looks forward to retiring at some point to pursue new activities and time with her husband and grandchildren.

Morgan Brett: Morgan and her extended family are part of what I would call our community family. Morgan was born twenty days before our son Gregory, and we have lived in the same neighborhood as the Brett's pretty much our whole lives. When we learned that Morgan was an aspiring editor, we excitedly invited her to edit this book to give her practical experience as part of her career path. We wish Morgan the best in her endeavors and hope this experience provided an exciting window into what will be, undoubtedly, a successful future. **About Morgan**: She is currently an English Literature major at Stony Brook University. She works part-time at the Port Jefferson Free Library, and ultimately aspires to be a professional editor. She is thankful that Doreen gave her the experience and opportunity to help edit this book. She will graduate with her Bachelor's in spring 2014.

Jean Rose Castiglione: Also known as JR, Jean Rose is a registered nurse who has worked in the health field for forty years. She resides in Miller Place, NY with her husband, Robert of thirty-eight years and youngest daughter, Livia. She has recently welcomed her father into her home after the passing of her loving mother. JR also has two older, married daughters, one who lives in Ohio and the other in Las Vegas.

Brian Cohen: With business experience beginning in 1983, matched with a desire which began in 2006 to become a more dynamic speaker, Brian found his true passion. He brings together the knowledge of the business world and the effectiveness of communication in his company, Strategies of Success. Brian hosts and produces a variety of television and podcast radio shows. Brian is also a partner at Comedy to Go, a company that produces comedy fundraisers. He offers classes to comedians and business people who want to improve their communications skills and works with Recovery Comics with Keith Richard to encourage people in alcohol and substance abuse recovery.

Ruth Curran: Ruth's passion and area of intense study and exploration has been the connection between the brain and daily functioning, in particular what happens to this connection as a result of aging and disease/injury. This fascination spurred her latest project, craniumcrunches.com, a photo-based series of thinking puzzles and games that help work around the effects of age, disease, or injury (TBI) on cognitive functioning and quality of life. Ms. Curran's primary focus is using a wide variety of games, those that inspire players to imagine, use strategies, and focus to succeed, as a path to better thinking, better functioning, and better quality of life.

Laurence Dresner: Mr. Dresner is a Chartered Financial Consultant (ChFC), a designation conferred on individuals who have passed a rigorous series of comprehensive tests and maintain annual continuing education requirements. He has been a financial planner since 1990 and a tax preparer since 1999. Mr. Dresner has also authored the book *Personal Finance for Clergy*, is a columnist, public speaker, teacher and has served as a not for profit board member. His articles have appeared in Financial Planning Magazine, the Journal of Practical Estate Planning, local newspapers, and web sites. Mr. Dresner is a member of Toastmasters International and several financial industry organizations including the Financial Planning Association (FPA) and National Association of Tax Professionals (NATP). Prior to being a financial planner, Laurence was a music composer for theatre and cabaret in New York City. He has a master's degree in music from the New England Conservatory of Music, and bachelor degrees in music and business communications from SUNY. He is the proud father of his incredible children Rebecca and Stephen.

Laura Francomano Facini: Laura is co-president of Freehand Graphics, Inc. of Holbrook, New York. Along with her husband Charlie, Freehand was established in 1982 as a graphics firm for their textile printing company. After selling the textile firm in the early '90s, Freehand Graphics expanded into a design and consulting company and in 1995 launched its first graphics software for the screen-printing industry. The company focus has shifted to software and product development. Laura has worked in numerous facets of the company including design and product marketing, international reseller management, and sales. She attended the University of Florida, Gainesville for two years then four years at the School of Visual Arts in New York, NY where she earned a Bachelor of Fine Arts in Graphic Design. Laura is the mother of Samantha and Valerie.

Joseph Farina: For over a decade, Joe has been recognized as a talented personal trainer and business owner. His experiences, starting at the age of twenty-two, ranged from retail stores to online distribution in the health and wellness field. After leaving the world of business, Joe turned his sights to law enforcement to fulfill a childhood dream. Joe took that dream and graduated ranked number one in his academy class. Not long after his career in law enforcement began, the world of the entrepreneur came calling again. This time he found the industry of network marketing, or as he says, "Network marketing found me." He became a fast study of the industry and has quickly become a rising leader in his field. With the same drive and passion that led him back to the life of an entrepreneur, Joe also found his place as a motivational speaker and explosive trainer in the art of personal development. Joe has been awarded recognition for his speaking by Toastmasters International and is quickly gaining a reputation in speaking circles as a guy whose speeches are, "So hot they light water on fire." Born in Spring Mount, Pennsylvania, Joe now resides in New Jersey with his lovely wife, Janelle.

Keith Richard Godwin: Keith is an honorably discharged Marine. He is a Certified Alcohol and Substance Abuse Counselor who works per-diem at a crisis center and full-time as an addictions therapist at a VA hospital. Keith has worked with the Special Olympics and notes that one of the most personally rewarding times of his life was working for an organization that cared for the developmentally disabled. Keith is the founder and co-owner of a comedy business, Comedy to Go, which provides fundraisers and entertainment anywhere, at anytime. He also started his own recovery comedy division called recoverycomic.com, which is comedy geared for people in some type of recovery. Keith is happily married to his beautiful wife Annmarie. They own a diva shi-poo named Giggles, who he loves to death.

Christine Guma: Chrissy resides in North Carolina with her husband, Tommy, her son Andrew and her mother. Her new career enables her to help others provide for themselves when facing a health crisis. Chrissy has been very active in her community and has conducted many events and fund-raisers. She is a positive thinking advocate, always ready to lend a helping hand to others. Chrissy is also one of Doreen's favorite sister-in-laws!

Matthew Gelber: Dr. Gelber is a clinical psycho-therapist with a master's in clinical counseling psychology. He is a graduate of the University of New York at Stony Brook, Chestnut Hill College in Philadelphia, and Eagleville Hospital in Montgomery County. He is the president and founder of The Weldon Center Malvern, a counseling and therapy center developed for exploring all aspects of psychology. Matthew writes for a number of publications and has received the Top Psychotherapist, Top Doc and People's choice award from *Main Line Today* magazine. Matthew is a member of the American Psychology Association and the Pennsylvania Marriage and Family Association. He and his wife, an Ob/Gyn doctor, are proud parents of twins. Matthew is a charter member of the Chester County Chamber of Business and Industry and works closely with the community to inspire mental health understanding. He speaks at schools and companies in the area to encourage mental health awareness.

Christie Korth: Christie is a Crohn's disease survivor, author, certified health coach and holistic nutritionist who found her way to health and wellness after nearly succumbing to a severe case of Crohn's disease. After harnessing the power of nutrition and gaining her health back, she went on to become the founder and director of Happy & Healthy Wellness Counseling based just outside of New York City. She studied at the Institute for Integrative Nutrition, Columbia University and the Clayton College of Natural Health and is a Certified Holistic Health Practitioner with the American Association of Drugless Practitioners. Christie is the Corporate Director of Nutrition for Brain Balance Achievement Centers, where she designs the nutrition protocols for their franchises across the country. Christie is a nutrition expert for Dr. Oz's Sharecare.com and frequently contributes nutrition articles to magazines. She is the author of the *IBD Healing Plan and Recipe Book*. Christie lives in New York with her son, her husband, and their cat.

Heidi Krantz: Heidi is a Professional Life Coach and the founder of her company, Reinvention Life Coaching. Heidi draws upon her personal and professional experience to coach men and women through any phase of divorce or post-divorce. Heidi's coaching focuses on navigating all of the life changes that accompany divorce, including finding and cultivating new love, and her positive processes results in her client's development of strength, confidence, and success. Heidi has emerged as a New York area expert on "Moving-On", writing for various publications, serving as an expert panelist, and offering interactive seminars on a variety of topics including enhancing communication skills, goal setting, and dating success. Her groups empower many to shift into a more positive consciousness and to create opportunity during this challenging life transition. Heidi coaches her clients and workshop participants in person, via telephone, or via Skype Video. She lives in Long Island with her beloved husband and daughter. Heidi is very proud of her three adult children and their wonderful spouses.

Jeffrey Levy: Jeff is president of Janusian Insights Inc., a management consultant firm that introduces leaders and managers to a way of thinking and communicating that stimulates continuous strengthening. His simple yet powerful process enables change from the way we currently view the world, from solving problems and fixing things to seeking the best of human potential. Jeff believes that we need to reinvent the way workplaces work to uncover new opportunities and expand horizons into corporate culture, values, human behavior, leadership, vision creation, and business growth. In previous years, Jeff has held a variety of executive positions in such organizations as Citigroup, TSI Communications Worldwide, Leadership Solutions Metro, and Dale Carnegie. He holds a bachelors degree in marketing, and has been active in the not-for-profit community for many years. He is active on many Boards and not for profit organizations.

Rebecca L. Norrington: Rebecca is first and foremost a student of the Universe and ITs Laws. She has a Bachelor of Science degree in Psychology, along with decades of education and training on topics from Spirituality to Human Behavior. Her professional journey includes several vocations: Speaker, Author, Spiritual Teacher, Radio Host and Certified Fitness Instructor. In August 2011, Rebecca premiered her online radio show RealitySpirituality. Rebecca shares revolutionary tools and strategies that enable people to maintain and sustain a personal vibration of internal peace and contentment, regardless of external circumstances. RealitySpirituality focuses on everyday events and how these events affect our personal vibration. Rebecca writes at rebeccanorrington.com.

Tami Racaniello: Tami is a certified personal trainer and fitness instructor, holistic nutritional consultant, wellness coach, reiki master, writer, speaker and raw food chef. At the age of forty, Tami realized her path was destructive to her health and well-being. Making changes to her mindset and lifestyle led to a personal weight loss of 130 pounds. Tami's techniques and teachings have helped many to achieve better health and better quality of life. She is the President of It's Time to Get Fit, Inc.

Works Cited in Order of Appearance

꩜

[1] Peale, Norman Vincent. *Page 151. The Power of Positive Thinking*. New York: Fireside/Simon & Schuster, 2003. 151. Print.

[2] "It Ain't About How Hard You Hit from Rocky Balboa (2006)." *Samplage*. Samplage, n.d. Web. 26 Feb. 2013. <http://samplage.com/movie-quotes/it-aint-about-how-hard-you-hit>.

[3] Averbach, Leo. "Second and Third Marriages Are Failing at an Alarming Rate." *Huffington Post*. N.p., 31 Mar. 2012. Web. 17 Feb. 2013.

[4] Yen, Hope. "New Formula Finds More Americans in Poverty." *www.boston.com*. N.p. 6 Jan. 2011. Web. 10 Mar. 2013.

[5] "Suicide in the U.S.: Statistics and Prevention." *NIMH RSS*. National Institute of Mental Health, n.d. Web. 1 June 2012.

[6] "An Estimated 1 in 10 U.S. Adults Report Depression." *Centers for Disease Control and Prevention*. Centers for Disease Control and Prevention, 31 Mar. 2011. Web. 1 June 2012.

[7] "Major Depressive Disorder in Children." *NIMH RSS*. National Institute of Mental Health, n.d. Web. 1 June 2012.

[8] Wilmington, Harold. *Wilmington's Guide to the Bible*. Wheaton: Tyndale House Publishers, 1984

[9] NIDDIC. "National Digestive Diseases Information Clearinghouse (NDDIC)." *Digestive Diseases Statistics for the United States*. US Department of Health and Human Services, June 2010. Web. 12 Mar. 2013.

[10] Landau, Elizabeth. "Health Care Costs to Bulge along with U.S. Waistlines." *CNN*. Cable News Network, 01 Jan. 1970. Web. 15 Mar. 2013.

[11] Lopatto, Elizabeth. "Life Expectancy in the U.S. Drops for First Time Since 1993, Report Says." *Bloomberg*. Bloomberg.com, 9 Dec. 2010. Web. 15 Mar. 2013.

[12] Roth, J.D. "George Kinder: Three Questions about Life Planning." *Get Rich Slowly â€" Personal Finance That Makes Sense*. GetRichSlowly.org, 15 Feb. 2009. Web. 4 Mar. 2013.

[13] Fleming, Julie. "The Power of Habit." *Innovate*. Lex Innova Consulting, 28 Mar. 2012. Web. 3 Mar. 2013.

About the Author

Doreen Guma, MA, FACHE, CPC, CLC

꧁❀꧂

*D*oreen believes a lot of us have said it, "If I knew then what I know now," and is excited to finally see this book come to fruition. A vision that started nine years ago in 2004, Doreen asked others, including family, friends and professionals from her website, www.TimetoPlay.com to contribute their stories. Doreen and the contributors have graciously shared heartfelt stories about what they've learned through life lessons and trial and error. This book is a compilation of their experiences: things they have done, what they have learned, and observations they have made, with the hope someone will recognize themselves in their stories and spark a change to make their lives better.

Doreen has worked in healthcare since 1987. Tired of seeing the "sick and sad", she founded Time to Play, *Resources for a Better Life*, and www.timetoplay.com. Time to Play is her dream to bring resources to others so they can learn what they need to know and enjoy life. Doreen's mantra is "people helping people". Her goal and the goal of her team is to provide content in a non-threatening manner and to introduce a proactive approach vs. reactive thinking. Doreen is also the founder of the BExtraordinary™ makeup line with the goal to re-empower others by reminding them to BExtraordinary™ !

Doreen holds a Bachelor of Science in Management, a Masters in Business and Policy Studies, is a Fellow of the American College of Healthcare Executives (a board certified healthcare executive), a Certified Professional Coach and a Certified Life Coach. Doreen worked in administration in a hospital and as the Director of Quality Improvement, Risk Manager and Director of Medical Records in a skilled nursing home. Since 2005, she and her husband have owned D. James Marketing, a healthcare specific marketing firm which assists healthcare organizations with new program generation, quality improvement, staff and client satisfaction, event coordination and coordinating educational symposiums.

After her father abandoned their family when she was seventeen, Doreen made some choices, explained in her chapters, where she made some things in her life harder than they had to be. She wished she had someone that could have snapped her back into reality. She shares her observations and opinions based on her own experience, not to preach to others, but to tell her story.

Doreen lives on Long Island with her loving husband James of 25 years, their three children, Gregory, Nicholas and Jacquelyn, their dog Cody and their fish. She continues on her quest for quality of life and relearning how to enjoy life.

CPSIA information can be obtained at www.ICGtesting.com
Printed in the USA
BVOW07s1418131213

338979BV00001B/1/P